HOW TO
WIN
ONE
MILLION
DOLLARS

and shit glitter

This novel is based on real-life events. However, some names
and identifying details have been changed to protect the
privacy of those involved. The story has been only lightly
fictionalized for these purposes.

www.howtowinonemilliondollars.com

Written and Illsutrated by:
Luke Stoffel

Developmental Editors:
Cassandra Vann and Laura von Holt

Advisors:
Kate Love, Jamie Barry, and Ben Boven

Special Thanks to:
My family: Joyce, Willy, Jess, Heidi, Dan, & Bill Stoffel.
And my partners in crime Jill, Tom & Joyce Connors,
Jenni Wittman, Sue Riedel, Bill & Deb Fordice,
Cyndi Gryte, Alys Arden, Jerry Wong, Chenny Ang,
Thitiya Chongvanich, Ade Pratama, Jackie Nittayarot,
Carrie Seim, and Kim Hale for riding this crazy ride
called life with me.

Audiobook Performed by:
Patrick Mealey

Editoral Assistant and Copy Editing by:
OpenAI / ChatGPT

SLIPPER

Slipper Books - An Imprint of Cinderly Press

In dedication to:
Ethan Adi Guidjaja

I'd especially like to thank
**Laura von Holt, Daniel Beaver-Seitz, and
the writing group at Middle Collegiate Church**
for their support in helping me craft these deeply
personal stories over the years, and through a
crushing pandemic.

None of this would have been possible without
your hearts, time, and compassion.

- Luke

HOW TO WIN ONE
MILLION
DOLLARS
and shit glitter

Table of Contents:

Warning: May cause feelings...

Heads up! This story delves into bullying, learning disabilities, LGBTQ+ relationships, illness, and the role of using technology to overcome obstacles—all handled with humor, honesty, and a lot of heart. So, with that out of the way—ready to dive in? Let's make a deal...

"If you are a dreamer, a wisher,
a liar, a hope-er, a pray-er, a magic
bean buyer... If you're a pretender
come sit by my fire."

Where the Sidewalk Ends
- Shel Silverstein -

Congratulations!
You've been awarded a gold star
for reading this book!

Redeem this page for a free personal pan pizza
at any participating Pizza Hut!*

The Book It! program was inspired by President Ronald Reagan's call for American businesses to get involved in education. Students were rewarded with a free Personal Pan Pizza for reaching their reading goals. The program was available to pre-K through sixth grade classrooms. It was a national phenomenon and was considered the largest and longest-running corporate supported reading program.

If I told you how much free pizza I ate as a kid, you wouldn't believe me for a second!

*This offer expires 3/31/1985

How To Win a Million Dollars

Note from the author:
A Cautionary Fairytale

If you picked up this book hoping to learn the secret to winning a million dollars, well, you might be in for a surprise. And if you've made it this far without turning back for a refund, I admire your optimism—but you still have time to hand this book back to the clerk and get your money back. I won't be mad. In fact, I'll admire your hustle. But I'm not going to lie to you—at least, not in the prologue. The pages ahead are a (99.9%) true account of my misadventures—it is reality with a fistful of fairy dust.

I wasn't alone in writing this. You see, every good scheme needs a partner-in-crime—someone in the background who doesn't mind getting their hands dirty, someone who can see the big picture even when the details start to blur. Along the way, I had a silent accomplice, a co-conspirator. No, not a ghostwriter (I wrote all these stories myself)—more like a fellow hustler of sorts. This accomplice, whom you'll meet later, helped me shape the wild, disconnected threads of my thoughts into something worth reading, a voice that kept me grounded in my delusions while maintaining my quirky, chaotic go-getter yet charming writing style. A cheerleader and editor, someone who, in my darkest moments, told me I was funny. "Hey, maybe you're not crazy after all... or maybe you are, but in a good way."

So here we are: me, my tangled stories, and you holding the finished product of a collaboration that involved more trial and error than I care to admit. I've spent years rewriting these stories, attending classes, reading them aloud to groups, and the truth is, they're not just about schemes to make a quick buck—they're about trying to find my way through life's unexpected hurdles.

Back in school, my teachers were convinced I wasn't trying hard enough. C, C+, D—"Luke, you can do better than this." Turns out, I wasn't lazy; I just had undiagnosed dyslexia. But it was the 1980s— my mom's idea of a diet was butter on white bread for lunch. We didn't know anything. We didn't even have a word for what I was struggling through.

No one spells out for you how to legitimately win a million dollars. It's not possible. The YouTuber who says he can is just taking your money. (I know, I paid him.) There are soooo many roadblocks waiting for you when you're chasing that million-dollar dream. We were all sold a sugar-coated lie—work hard, play by the rules, and success will fall into your lap. Sure, maybe for a handful of folks. But for the rest of us? We're stuck navigating invisible obstacles, hoping we don't trip over the next one. Personally, I've found I'm more prosperous when I lie, cheat, and steal.

This isn't a "pull yourself up by the bootstraps" kind of story. That story is a lie. This is about the hustle—the real kind. The one that involves getting knocked down, dusting yourself off, and figuring out the next move. It's about questioning the system because while the world might love a Cinderella story, most of us are stuck scrubbing the floors (or a urinal) without a fairy godmother in sight.

But I won't spoil the whole plot here in the prologue. Let's just say, I'm okay with you not liking me by the end of the book—some of my closest friends could barely look me in the eye after they finished. "You can't do that!" they said. But I can, actually, and that's the deal I'm making with myself, and with you, the reader. Let's shake on that. If you're ready for an adventure full of ridiculous, madcap schemes and heartfelt confessions, and if you're willing to let this bright-eyed, unreliable narrator drag you into a harebrained catastrophe, then strap in—because we're in for a bumpy ride!

Once upon a time, in a kingdom far, far away from long, long ago... there lived a boy, a fireplace full of ash, and a pair of young, soot-filled hands full of singed, smoldering, rescued dreams. But unlike other fairytales, this one wasn't about finding princes or glass slippers—yet. No, this kid had his eyes set on something much, much bigger...

Chapter 1
Cereal Entrepreneur

The first time I tried to win a million dollars, it was the sweltering summer of 1985, and the Mississippi River was swollen and threatening to spill over its banks. The town was on edge, but thanks to the giant quarry wall my grandpa helped build back in the '50s, we were safe from the river's fury. It was during that unforgettable summer when Cap'n Crunch went missing, and panic spread across the nation like wildfire.

Supermarkets were packed with towering displays of Cap'n Crunch, a mountain of yellow and blue boxes stretching to the ceiling. But when you looked up, there was no Captain. His jovial face had vanished, leaving behind nothing but dotted lines and a big question mark. He had disappeared, zeroed out. *Zoinks!* What was I to do?

The commercials made it sound so simple: find the Captain, restore him to his cereal kingdom, and win ONE MILLION DOLLARS. For a kid like me, the stakes couldn't have been higher. A million dollars wasn't just a number—it was a golden ticket, a way out of this tiny Mississippi River town.

Every Saturday morning, I'd sit in my parents' living room—a shrine to America's Bicentennial celebration. The royal blue carpet stretched wall to wall, its plush fibers worn thin in front of the TV. A deep red couch commanded the room like a throne, while gold curtains depicting Revolutionary War scenes framed the windows. It was like 1776 had crashed into 1980s suburbia, and somehow, we were still stuck suspended in between.

As my brothers and sisters tormented each other in the background, I was glued to the TV. The old box hummed as commercials blared, demanding kids like me solve the mystery, save the Captain, and claim the prize. The urgency of it all buzzed in my chest, electrifying the air around me. To a seven-year-old like me, a million dollars wasn't just thrilling—it was everything. It meant a chance to escape this town, this life, and find something more.

In the afternoons, when the noise at home became too much, I'd head for the bluffs. The familiar path wound through tall grass that swayed gently in the breeze, the green hills rolling endlessly toward the horizon. I'd climb to my favorite perch and sit there for hours, the town spread out below me like a miniature toy train set. The limestone clock tower stood proudly at the center, surrounded by the river, the factories, and the steeples of the churches. Everything looked so small from up here, but somehow, it felt even smaller at eye level.

You see, up close, the town was just a second-rate version of Main Street USA, stripped of all the charm and magic of Disneyland. Most of the families here were like mine—working-class and stuck. I lived on the North End, what people would call the wrong side of the tracks, where factory workers like my dad scraped by.

I was a short, scrawny kid with wavy dishwater blond hair, wearing tattered dungaree shorts that were practically a second skin during the summer, their faded denim streaked with dirt and grass stains. My skin was golden tan from hours in the sun, but my legs were a patchwork of scars from chigger bites I couldn't stop picking. Sitting cross-legged on the warm earth, absently scratching at the bites, my mind churned, methodically piecing together a plan. The Captain was missing. My ticket to freedom was hidden somewhere out there, and all I had to do was find it. Yet from this vantage point, the possibility of something greater still felt wildly out of reach. A million dollars meant escape, and as I sat on that bluff, staring out at the endless rows of cornfields, I swore to myself I was going to find it.

Each week, I'd beg my mom to let me tag along to the grocery store. Econofoods smelled like a strange mix of fresh produce and fake lemon cleaning products that clung to the air. The linoleum floors were scuffed and worn down from years of shopping carts rattling over them and the steady shuffle of feet. Jess, my five-year-old sister, was always a whirlwind of energy, darting between aisles like a tiny tornado. She had our dad's button nose and her favorite white, frilly cotton top tucked into neatly pressed khaki shorts. Her tiny diamond stud earrings, pierced at Claire's in the mall when she was a baby, sparkled as she twirled through the store. Her short brown pixie cut bobbed with every step, her energy infectiously lighthearted even as I plotted my next move.

Mom was anything but calm—she was a peacock in human form. With her siren-red lips and cheeks always blushed a rosy pink to match, she strutted through the store, making sure to chat up every neighbor on her way. Her raven-black hair, all done up in a beehive, was straight out of the '60s and still undeniably chic. Her gold bangle bracelets would rattle down the aisles, clinking against the cuffs of her puff-sleeved denim jacket with shoulder pads, over a matching jean skirt, exuding a presence that was bold and full of life. She pushed the cart with flair, her vibrant energy filling the frozen section with heat as Jess twirled around her, while I, laser-focused on my mission, pleaded for Cap'n Crunch like my life depended on it.

"Please, Mom, we need Cap'n Crunch! Please!"

I tugged at her hand, whined, threw tantrums. I knew that inside each box was a clue—a piece of the puzzle that could lead to the Captain's whereabouts. Every box came with a detective kit, complete with a badge and instructions on how to dial a 1-800 number, punch in the codes, and get the next clue. It was life-or-death for me. My mom, however, wasn't having it. After two weeks of my non-stop bellyaching, she stopped taking me to the store altogether. I would have ripped open every box in the place if I could, but she wasn't giving me the chance.

Still, every week, she brought home a family-sized box of Cap'n Crunch, and I ate nothing but that cereal all summer. By the fourth week of the contest, things were looking grim. I'd gone through three boxes already, and I was well into my fourth, but I didn't have nearly enough clues to track down the Captain. I was starting to get sick of the peanut-buttery crunch that I once loved. My mom refused to buy more unless I finished every last Crunch Berry in the house, but I had to find another way. There was no quitting. I needed more boxes.

Jess and I—two mischievous, determined kids—came up with a plan. We started pestering our mom to visit every relative we could think of: Grandma, our aunts, uncles, cousins, anyone. Our real motive was simple: we'd sneak into their kitchens and raid their pantries for Cap'n Crunch boxes. Jess, always in on my schemes, would distract the adults with her wild energy, twirling around their legs, while I rummaged through cabinets.

But, surprisingly, this brilliant plan didn't work out as well as we'd hoped. Apparently, old people didn't stock Cap'n Crunch. Who knew?

So we took things up a notch. Jess and I began running up and down our narrow street, knocking on the doors of the most unlikely neighbors. Some houses we rarely approached, like Mr. O'Brien's with its creaky screened-in porch or Mrs. Connors' with her massive greenhouse that always smelled like wet dirt. And then there was Mrs. Hansen, who had a tiny, yappy Maltese dog that I loathed. The little beast would bark its head off at us, baring its tiny sharp teeth and making ferocious faces through the glass. It made my skin crawl every time, but we weren't about to be scared off by some obnoxious dog.

"Do you have any Cap'n Crunch?" we'd ask, standing in doorways with wide, innocent eyes.

No one did. It was disheartening to find that random elderly people didn't typically keep sugary cereal on hand. Undeterred, we decided to expand our operation. We recruited neighborhood kids, promising them a cut of the million dollars if they could get their hands on those beautiful blue and gold boxes of Crunch Berries. They eagerly joined the scheme, asking their parents, uncles, and grandparents for boxes and calling us the moment they got one.

We huddled around the phone like it was some magical artifact, fingers trembling as we punched in codes from our stash of cereal boxes. Each time, the ritual was the same: the phone would buzz, ring, and then—BEEP! Jess and I would hold our breath, hearts pounding with anticipation. We waited, almost daring the universe to reward our clever scheming with the golden clue that would lead us to the Captain.

But more often than not, the only response was the dull tone of disappointment. A wrong code. A dead end. Or worse—silence. We'd hang up, punch in another code, and try again. The clues were as scattered and random as the cereal pieces floating in our bowls every morning. Some were completely useless, cryptic nonsense that didn't get us anywhere. Others led us in circles. We were grasping at straws, and with each failed call, the excitement that once buzzed around us started to fizzle out.

At first, the neighborhood kids were right there with us—just as invested, as hungry for that million-dollar prize. They'd show up at our house, boxes in hand, eager to be part of the big win. We'd hype them up, promising, "This is it! This time we'll find him!" But as August dragged on and clue after clue led to nowhere, our little army of detectives began to lose faith. Their enthusiasm wilted like the summer heat. One by one, they drifted away, off to other summer distractions that didn't involve scouring cereal boxes for a ghostly captain.

But not Jess and me. We kept at it. We were determined (okay, I was determined—Jess? Maybe, she was just along for the ride). Me, the seven-year-old mastermind, and Jess, my trusty sidekick, who was starting to get skeptical. She'd sit there diligently next to her big brother, her pixie-cut hair falling into her eyes, gnawing on her lip as we dialed the 1-800 number again and again. Her usual wild energy had dimmed, replaced with quiet anticipation that, over time, shifted to thinly veiled frustration.

"Luke," she said one day, as we stared at yet another disappointing clue, "what if we never find him? What if... what if the Captain doesn't want to be found?"

I looked at her, refusing to believe it. "No, Jess. We're close. We have to be close."

But deep down, I knew she was right. As the summer wore on, so did the reality that our grand scheme wasn't going to end with us as millionaires.

And then came the final blow—the crushing truth we hadn't wanted to face. One morning, while swirling around our pink-tinted milk from soggy Crunch Berries, we stumbled upon the fine print on the back of the box.

We read it together, our faces growing pale as the words sank in: General Mills wasn't giving out a million dollars to one lucky kid. No, they were giving away a measly $100 to 10,000 kids.

One hundred dollars?! I slumped back into my chair, staring at the paper in disbelief. Jess, wide-eyed, looked at me for reassurance, but what could I say? The game was rigged from the start, and we had been played. All those hours spent dialing numbers, tearing through boxes, making deals with neighborhood kids—it had all been for nothing.

"WHAT?" I finally exploded, fists clenching. "A hundred dollars? That's it? What am I supposed to do with a hundred dollars?!"

Jess nodded furiously, crossing her arms with the indignation only a five-year-old could muster. "A hundred dollars? That won't even buy us new bikes!"

We felt cheated, betrayed. Like someone had dangled the key to our freedom right in front of our noses, only to yank it away at the last second. The Captain, that grinning face on the cereal box, felt more like a villain now. We glared at his image as though he had personally duped us.

The neighborhood kids, those who had stuck around for the ride, abandoned ship. They shrugged off the whole adventure like it had been a fun distraction, moving on to the next game of the summer. But for Jess and me, it was more than that. We had believed—truly believed—we could change everything. A million dollars would've bought us new bikes, sure, but it would've bought us a new life, a ticket out of this small-town dead end.

I remember slumping in my chair that afternoon, defeated. I swore I'd never touch another Crunch Berry as long as I lived. But as the frustration began to wear off, something else took its place—a kind of defiant determination. I might have been a kid, but I wasn't about to let this one failure crush my dreams. The Captain may have let us down, but I knew there had to be something else, something bigger waiting out there for me.

That summer, I learned a hard lesson: sometimes, the world doesn't deliver on its promises. Sometimes, the prize you're chasing turns out to be nothing more than a cardboard fantasy. But that didn't mean I was giving up. Not by a long shot. If there was one thing that summer had taught me, it was that there was something more out there for me—a ticket to something bigger and better than Crunch Berries. And I was going to find it, no matter how many schemes it took.

Back in the '80s, the world felt big. And I don't just mean the mall bangs and massive hair or the fact that our dad's white Oldsmobile looked like a land yacht. No, it was the whole vibe— the idea that all you needed was a little grit, a few schemes, and, according to President Ronald Reagan, a good dose of bootstrapping to get rich. Even at seven, I knew a million dollars could solve all your problems. That's what they told us in every TV commercial, sitcom, and radio show. Heck, even the president made it sound like wealth would trickle down from the clouds if you had enough of that good ol' American spirit.

But growing up, I didn't fully grasp the plainness of our middle-class life. To me, our world was normal, and it took years to realize what that meant. My dad worked at John Deere, building tractors a mile away from our house. He spent his days in the foundry, working with molten metal, welding parts beneath the tractor line. In my imagination, it was a fiery hellscape, with rivers of lava pouring down from towering machines—though the reality was probably only half as bad. Still, I can vividly recall him trudging up the gravel alleyway behind our house at the end of each shift, his slim but strong frame covered in silt from the factory floor. His tousled brown hair was always a mess, and his face carried the exhaustion of another long day in the trenches. He hated that job, loathed every minute of it.

But for every five years my dad worked in that foundry, he could shave one year off his 30-year sentence—I mean, contract—and qualify for early retirement. And he lasted years down there. He retired when I was ten, and he's been retired ever since—longer now than the time he spent at that factory. With his newfound freedom, Dad took to biking. He'd bike from California to Florida, dipping his tires in both the Pacific and Atlantic, or ride straight down the Continental Divide, the Rocky Mountains looming around him like sentinels. He went from being a blue-collar worker, hating every day of it, to living life the way he wanted. That drive to break free was something I admired in him. In a town like Dubuque, where nearly everyone had the same factory job, my dad's escape seemed like a miracle.

He'd landed the job at John Deere because my grandfather ran a small trucking company, hauling cattle and other goods back and forth along the rural highways of Iowa. For my dad, there was no way he was following in those footsteps. Escaping Rickardsville, a tiny town of forty people, was his first big win. In the '60s, getting hired at John Deere was like striking gold. Full health insurance, a pension, and retirement—all you had to trade was thirty years of your life, shoveling what my dad called "hell." But to him, thirty years of hell was worth the rest of his life in freedom. That desire to escape was a trait passed down in our family like an inheritance.

It wasn't always easy, though. Dad was in the union, and the guys running the factory were always trying to squeeze the little guy. He and his union buddies would go on strike, fighting for what they deserved. The unions ran our small town, even while Reagan was trying to bust them up. And I remember one summer when the strike dragged on, and we had to go on food stamps. To me, it was a strange kind of magic. I remember standing in the grocery store with my mom and Jess, holding those little coupons, and half of the groceries we loaded into the cart were free. It felt like we'd hit the jackpot, especially since Jess and I finally got to help pick out Fruit

Roll-Ups—our ultimate prize. But that illusion of luxury shattered at dinnertime. We'd sit down to what Jess and I called "toenail soup"—thin, watery, and smelling vaguely of government-issued meat. I realized that we weren't as well-off as I had thought. No amount of Fruit Roll-Ups could change that fact.

Mom wasn't one to shy away from making sure we kept our dignity, though. She strutted around our small three-bedroom house like it was her kingdom, Virginia Slim in hand, smoke curling around her delicate fingers, skirt swishing as she went about her day, never letting the stress show too much. The kitchen was her domain, with its gleaming white cabinets and cherry-red countertops, flecks of quartz catching the light like tiny stars—a reminder that even in the ordinary, there was always room for a little sparkle. That need to shine seeped into everything she did, from her perfectly frosted sugar cookies to the way she carried herself. And in ways I wouldn't fully realize until later, it seeped into us kids too, weaving a glittering thread that tied us together.

It was in that very kitchen, back in 1978, that she stood, trying to explain to my dad that she was pregnant with me—a big surprise, since my three older siblings were already teenagers. I was just a zygote in the womb, far too young to remember, but the story had become family lore. Dad had been furious, shouting and cursing, pacing back and forth like an umpire preparing to throw someone out of the game. He was a good man, but when life threw him a curveball, you had to watch out.

Fast forward three short years, and the scene repeated itself, only this time, the tension was thicker. My mom stood in the middle of our cherry-colored kitchen again, her voice trying to soften the blow as she broke the news to my father that another baby was on the way—my baby sister Jess. It wasn't joy that filled the room—it was dread. We were already standing on the edge of poverty, and this news felt like another gust of wind ready to push us off the cliff.

My dad, thinking of the financial stress, didn't take it well. His brow furrowed, and his jaw clenched as he paced back and forth, throwing his hands in the air. "How are we supposed to do this?" he muttered, over and over, frustration pouring out of him like steam from a boiling pot. We weren't destitute yet, but it felt like the walls were closing in. The strikes at the factory had already pushed us to the brink, and now, this?

You see, our house on the bluffs wasn't extravagant by any means—a small white little thing with three bedrooms and a large porch—that we'd turn into a stage in the summers. In the front yard, a sweet little plum tree stood, forever dropping sticky fruit, its branches so full of bees in the summer you couldn't even climb it. It wasn't a lot, but it was ours.

I shared it with my four siblings. My oldest sister, Heidi—a true teen of the '80s with her bobbed black hair and bright pastels— looked the most like our mother. Then there were my two older brothers and Jess—the pack of us, five kids born across three decades. The Catholic Church's stance on contraception made sure of that. My parents were devout, and their faith shaped every part of our lives. College wasn't just an option; it was a mandate, even though they'd never been themselves. To them, sending us to college was the only way we'd ever thrive beyond Dubuque. They had faith in things they didn't fully understand, and looking back now, I realize that faith built the foundation for our futures.

By the time I turned seven, my mom had taken a job at Econo- Foods to help make ends meet. She started working in the bakery, doing what she did best—baking cinnamon rolls, decorating birthday cakes, and spreading joy one confection at a time. But it came at a cost. Her early mornings meant no more goodbye hugs before school, just a bowl of sugary cereal and our neighbor, Mrs. Connors, with her ever-present greenhouse, to usher us off to class.

It wasn't common for women in our small town to work full-time back then, but we needed every dollar. One kid was heading to college, and my younger sister was still wetting the bed. Financial stress hung thick in the air, as heavy as the humid summers rolling over the river. I didn't know all the details, but even as a kid, I could sense we were close to the edge. Winning a million dollars would have changed everything for us.

Life in the '70s and '80s wasn't like it is now. With my mom at work most mornings, Heidi, the oldest, was in charge. Our parents didn't hover—as long as we weren't hurt or in trouble with the law, we were left to figure things out on our own. I learned early how to blend into the background, quietly observing everything around me. My older brothers, on the other hand, were wild. With their rat tails and reckless attitudes, they'd sneak out at night and come home with stolen road signs or flags, laughing like they were invincible. Then there was my cousin, who lived with us for a while after being kicked out of her house. She'd steal money from my mom's purse during church, and when she got caught, she was asked to leave. All around me, people were pushing boundaries, and I quietly resolved to stay out of trouble.

Heidi, though, was the good one. She was inseparable from our neighbor Jill, who was skinny as a rail with shocking red hair and about 10,000 freckles. Jill felt like my third sister. Jess and I would spend weekends baking chocolate chip cookies with them in the kitchen. The most trouble Heidi and Jill ever got into was gossiping about the cute Catholic high school boys at the mall. Compared to the chaos around me, their harmless antics felt like a relief.

Still, Catholic school and Sunday Mass were non-negotiable. Heidi even went to a Catholic high school, where they had to attend church twice a week. The expectation was clear: be moral, be obedient, follow the rules. I remember once, when I was small, I stole a marble from a floral arrangement in a Yonkers department store. It was nothing—a tiny, iridescent flat marble—but the guilt swallowed me whole. I never confessed it to the priest, never told anyone. I hid it inside my Fievel Mousekewitz doll, where it stayed, a secret burden I carried for years.

But it wasn't just about avoiding the usual mischief. Deep down, I knew I was different, though I couldn't place why at the time. At seven years old, I knew nothing about sex or sexuality, but my burden felt bigger than petty theft or my siblings' rebellion. It felt like something that, if discovered, would never be forgiven. I needed to be perfect—the golden child. That's what was expected of me, and it's what I expected of myself. So, I kept my head down, blending in, while silently carrying the weight of it.

By the fall of 1988, Dad's strike at the factory had stretched on for months, and more strikes followed in the years after. My mom's meager income helped us scrape by, but the tension at home grew thicker with every passing week. Meanwhile, our neighbors, with their office jobs and seemingly cushy lives, didn't have to deal with the same strife. They never needed food stamps. We were scraping by, but they seemed untouched by the factory's struggles. The factory was the lifeblood of our town, but it also drained the spirit of every worker who toiled there.

Still, growing up, life was always a mix of scrapes and triumphs. None of us understood the full weight of it at the time. I didn't know that Dad's constant stress came from his fight to get us out. But I do remember the small victories—like sneaking Fruit Roll-Ups into the cart or dreaming of something bigger as Jess and I twirled through the grocery store aisles. Those moments of freedom were my first glimpse of what it meant to want more than we had.

As my sister went off to college, I began to see that there was another way. I wasn't going to follow in my dad's footsteps, working at the factory. I knew that much. The idea of spending my life working on an assembly line seemed unbearable to me—like it would slowly grind me down, the way it had my dad. He'd done what he had to for the family, but I was determined to find a different path.

My sister played piano, and it seemed like music and education were the key to escaping factory life. I dreamed of bigger things—climbing mountains, getting rich, being on TV. I longed to escape the confines of Dubuque, Iowa, and see the world beyond the Kennedy Mall. It was my sister's journey to college that opened my eyes to the possibilities that lay beyond the narrow world we lived in.

My family shared two newspaper routes like they were hand-me-down jeans. When it was our turn, Jess took the route that served the nursing home, while I, at ten years old, delivered newspapers up the bluff to the wealthier parts of town. I was making money now! It wasn't huge, but it was a start. My route included the condos overlooking the whole river valley—homes of the well-to-do, people who seemed a world away from our life. In my young eyes, that kind of lifestyle represented triumph, and I wanted it.

After school, Jess and I would hop on our bikes, ready to take on the world. The long hill behind our house was no match for us, not when we had a mission. From the top of that hill, the whole North End spread out beneath us like our personal kingdom. We could see everything—the hospital where I was born, the hilly cemetery where we said goodbye to Grandpa. It wasn't just a hill; it was a part of our daily life, a challenge we faced head-on. We'd huff and puff as we pedaled up, our legs burning with every push, but we were strong. Stronger than that hill, stronger than we knew. Every day, we dragged ourselves and our bikes up that steep incline, the effort shaping us into machines, toughened by the grind, ready to take on whatever the world threw our way. We weren't bound by those same rules. No, we had bigger dreams. I'd glance at Jess, her legs pumping furiously, her hair shooting out at odd angles from the climb. We weren't just delivering newspapers; we were hustling.

My bike—a glorious white beast with pink and purple splatter paint—had "Hustler" written boldly down the side in big letters, and it wasn't just a name; it was my mindset. That summer of 1988, I had dreams of making money, real money. And I wasn't alone. Every kid in town seemed to be scheming, but I knew my plan was different. It wasn't about scraping by; I was aiming for the big leagues. We had to get rich, and we had to get out.

That's when I found out about the McDonald's sweepstakes. That Sunday, every paper in America would come with a 45 vinyl record embedded in its pages, and if the chorus of kids on that record sang the entire McDonald's menu—perfectly—you'd win a million dollars. One million dollars! To me, that was still our golden ticket out of Iowa. One problem: we only got one record per household, and one record wasn't enough. But I had a plan—Jess and I would "borrow" the records from every single one of our 250 subscribers.

It was genius, really.

Sunday morning came, and the sun had barely cracked the horizon when we began our heist. We woke early, adrenaline buzzing in our veins. I hopped on the Hustler and pedaled up the bluff, wind whipping past my face, my heart racing with the thrill of it. My route was at the top, where the retired wealthy folks lived in their fancy condos, and I looked down at towering stacks of newspapers. The Sunday paper was thicker than usual—stacked more like Bibles on top of each other than the thin weekly Herald. I looked over my prize and attacked the stack like a pro. With every bundle I opened, I slipped out record after record—careful not to tear them, but not careful enough to prevent my actual job from looking completely disheveled. I did my best to reseal the papers like nothing had ever happened; I couldn't have my plot spoiled by someone calling in, asking why it looked like a tornado had hit their mailbox. Luckily, each record was made of slick plastic and, for the most part, slipped out easily. But tearing through hundreds of papers in the early dawn light wasn't easy by any means. By the time I had hit every house on my route, I had a stack of records as thick as the neighbor's yappy dog.

Heart pounding, I raced over to Jess's route at the nursing home, where she was wrapping up her side of the operation. The nursing home had its own set of challenges—people were always watching, even at that early hour. Jess had to be sneaky, slipping through unnoticed, with orderlies roaming the halls and residents peeking out of their rooms. But as I whipped into the parking lot and burst through the squeaky electric sliding doors, I spotted her—beaming, clutching a bundle of records like she'd struck gold. We locked eyes, and in that moment, we squealed, our laughter bouncing off the walls as we bolted out of the nursing home.

We tore through the streets, wind rushing past us as we sped back home, practically flying through the front door. We whizzed by our parents sitting at the kitchen table, drinking their coffee. I swear I saw the steam waver with our speed. They barely had time to part their lips, confused expressions forming as they began to ask what we were up to, but we were already gone, vanishing upstairs in a blur.

We locked ourselves in Jess's room, breathless with excitement, collapsing onto her pink shag carpet. The air was scented with candy perfume, but the anticipation was thick as we surrounded ourselves with our bounty—a glorious, glittering stash of 250 chances to strike gold. This was it. This was our moment.

Jess yanked out her little 45 record player from under the bed. The thing was ancient, but we didn't care. We set the first black disc on the spindle, and with a satisfying click, the needle dropped. The record began to spin, and our fate spun with it. The familiar jingle started—"Big Mac, McBLT, a Quarter Pounder with some cheese…" our hearts thudded in our chests as we waited for the magic.

But then—chaos. The chorus of kids stumbled over the words, their voices clashing into an indecipherable mess. "NO!" I screamed, yanking the record off, my fingers shaking with frustration.

"Let's try again," Jess said, determined. We grabbed another record, peeled off the backing, and tried again. *Big Mac, McBLT… a Quarter Pounder with some cheese, Filet-o-Fish, a hamburger, a cheeseburger, a Happy Meal, McNuggets, tasty golden fries, regular and larger sizes, a salad chef…* Then everything falls apart, the same jumble, the same disaster.

We were relentless. For hours, we sat hunched over the record player, peeling off record after record, our small hands working furiously to tear through all 250. By this point, I had memorized the entire menu myself! But the kids just sang the same chorus, ending with the same garbled voices—over and over. Each failure felt like a punch to the gut. Come on, just one perfect song! But it never came.

By the time the sun had crested the top of the bedroom window, casting the first golden rays through the cracks in Jess's curtains, we were completely spent. We collapsed onto her Strawberry Shortcake bedspread, staring up at the ceiling, too exhausted to speak. What had started as the heist of the century had turned into a colossal failure. Our biggest major hustle yet, and we hadn't even come close to success.

I sat up slowly, grabbing the last record, flipping it over to read the fine print on the back. There, in tiny, infuriating letters, was the final blow: you had to be 16 years old to even play, and the odds of the kids singing all the way through the menu were 1 in 80 million.

Jess groaned beside me, tossing a pillow over her face. "What? You mean we did all this for nothing?"

I let the record fall to the floor. "Yeah. It's all a sham."

We lay there in silence for a while, the sting of defeat settling over us. It wasn't the first time I had tried to make a million dollars, and deep down, I knew it wouldn't be the last. But still—this one hurt. All that effort, all that excitement, crushed under the weight of the fine print. But if I learned anything that summer, it was that the world didn't hand out million-dollar prizes easily.

I glanced at Jess, who peeked out from under her pillow, her face still red from the frustration. We hadn't won this time, but I wasn't about to give up. There was something bigger out there for us. And it sure as hell wasn't going to taste like Crunch Berries or a McBLT.

Then, my mom's voice boomed up the stairs. "Come on, kids! We're gonna be late for church!"

Zapped back into the real world, Jess groaned, and I let out a deep sigh. Not only would we have to sit through Sunday Mass in our disappointment, but we'd also have to silently beg God for forgiveness for all the "borrowing" we had done that morning. I could already picture it: kneeling in the pews, heads bowed, pretending to pray for good health and world peace when, really, we were praying for two things—one, that God would forgive us for ripping off all those records from old people, and two, that He'd still somehow send us that million dollars!

The passage of time had etched its mark on my life, but even after a few years, I was still diligently working the same paper route job, Jess and I saving every dollar we made for our college funds. The humdrum routine of delivering newspapers at the crack of dawn had settled into a rhythm, but little did we know, God had answered our prayers. A new opportunity shimmered tantalizingly on the horizon, ready to disrupt our ordinary world. This time, it wasn't Cap'n Crunch—it was something even bigger. McDonald's had done it again. They had unveiled the largest sweepstakes in American history: the first-ever Monopoly Sweepstakes.

The air was once again full of expectation that summer. Every McDonald's bag came with peel-and-stick Monopoly pieces, promising riches beyond our wildest dreams—new cars, jet skis, dream vacations. We needed to collect enough of the right pieces to fill the board and claim the jackpot. And to kick it all off, McDonald's had cleverly inserted Monopoly boards in every Sunday paper across the nation, each one with two free pieces.

My heart raced as I plotted out the plan. This was it. I could feel it. If God wasn't going to drop a million bucks straight into our laps, maybe we'd just have to hustle a little harder this time. I ran to Jess with the news, and her eyes lit up. She was in, no questions asked. Together, we were unstoppable.

Sunday morning arrived, and it felt like déjà vu. We woke up before dawn, adrenaline pumping, ready to strike. We hopped on our bikes and took off on the now-familiar route, stronger and faster than in our younger days, but now armed with an unwavering determination. The sun had barely risen, casting long shadows over the quiet streets. The air was cool, but I was already sweating, my hands twitching on the handlebars as we pedaled up that long, steep hill. The town lay below us, but all I could think about was the hundreds of newspapers waiting at the top, each one hiding that elusive ticket to freedom.

We tore into those stacks of Sunday papers with precision, just like we had years ago with the record fiasco. My hands flew through the bundles, ripping out the Monopoly boards, each new piece a glimmer of hope. In total, we had at least 500 chances between us—500 opportunities to get rich quick. I could barely contain my excitement. The thrill of it all was almost too much for my young heart to handle. I even sent up a quick prayer—a little something for luck.

By the time I finished my route, my knapsack bulged with Monopoly boards. I raced over to meet Jess, who was already done and standing at the edge of the parking lot, a huge grin on her face, clutching her own stash of pieces. "Let's go!" she yelled, and we took off for home, pedaling like our lives depended on it.

We barreled through the front door, nearly knocking over a chair as we sped past our parents, who were halfway through frying their morning eggs. They glanced at each other and rolled their eyes, knowing full well we were up to no good, when we were gone—two streaks of excitement racing up the stairs, hearts pounding.

Once in Jess's room, we dumped the entire haul onto the ever more shabby pink shag rug. The room practically sparkled with possibility. We sat cross-legged, our fingers twitching as we peeled off the stickers one by one, placing each piece carefully on the board. St. Charles Place. Oriental Avenue. St. Vincent's Place. The board slowly filled up as we sifted through our mountain of treasure, our excitement growing with every piece we stuck to the cardboard. The coveted Boardwalk square was still out there—our golden ticket to paradise.

But as the minutes ticked by, the pile of unpeeled stickers got smaller and smaller. My heart began to sink. We hadn't found Boardwalk. We hadn't found Park Place either. As I peeled the last sticker, my hand shook. I slapped it onto the board in frustration.

"The game is rigged!" I shouted, throwing my hands up in defeat. "It's a scam, just like last time!"

Jess looked up from her side of the pile, her face a mix of disappointment and exhaustion. "Are you sure? Maybe we missed something?"

"No," I said, shaking my head. "McDonald's isn't giving out millions. Not to kids like us. The winning piece is probably in some fancy McDonald's in New York or Los Angeles. No way it's here, in stupid little small-town Dubuque."

I was furious. After all the work we'd done—after all the pieces we'd collected—it felt like we were being cheated. The sting of the Cap'n Crunch debacle came rushing back, the failure with the records. The crushing reality of small-town life, where we were always a little too far from anything exciting, hit me all over again. I flopped back onto the bed, staring at the ceiling, tears welling in my eyes.

But Jess wasn't ready to give up. She reached into the pile of prizes we'd set aside—the free fries, the ice cream cones, the sodas—and tossed me one. "Well, one thing's for sure... we're rich in McDonald's food!" she said with a grin. As I looked at the floor, I realized she was right. All those discarded pieces we'd been carelessly tossing aside had tiny amounts of glory hidden in them—free mini prizes scattered everywhere.

We may not have won the million dollars, but we had a summer's worth of free food! Enough to treat half the neighborhood. And in that moment, I realized something: we'd beaten the system, in our own way. Maybe it wasn't the victory we'd been dreaming of, but it was still a win.

That summer, Jess and I didn't just score a handful of Happy Meals—we tapped into something bigger. The thrill of chasing small victories was part of a larger promise kids like us bought into, especially in the '80s. Reagan and his trickle-down economics plan—Reaganomics—wasn't just a reelection campaign slogan blaring on TV every Saturday morning; it was a million bucks waiting to be picked up off the ground. All I needed was the right sweepstakes, a McDonald's Monopoly piece, or maybe a Cap'n Crunch decoder ring to unlock it.

The whole country was vibing with that 'get rich quick' energy, like a nation of scrappy entrepreneurs. Ronald Reagan practically promised us that wealth would rain down from the top, so naturally, I figured if I stood in the right spot, I'd get drenched in it.

Chapter 2
Star Search

My childhood carried on, though the grand schemes that once fueled my days began to fade into the background. Jess and I, still partners in crime, had learned a thing or two about trusting "the man" after our McDonald's Monopoly days. I hadn't fully given up on the dream of gaming the system—I mean, once you get a taste for it, it sticks with you—but I was quickly realizing how easily we were all sold that sugar-coated dream. They promised kids like me a million dollars, sprinkled a little daydreaming into the mix, and boom, lifelong customer. But by the time junior high rolled around, I had a new enemy, and it wasn't McDonald's. It was reality itself.

Jess and I stayed low-key for a while. No big capers. Small things here and there. We tried to adopt a family of bunnies to breed and sell in the backyard, which, of course, didn't last long. One day, while I was knee-deep in rabbit shit, cleaning out the bins, I broke the gate. Poof—like a magic trick, they were gone. So, that was the end of that experiment. And don't even get me started on the hamster that seemed determined to escape his glass prison at every opportunity. I should've felt a sort of kinship with him, both of us trapped in one way or another. We named him Houdini because, from the very first day, he had one goal in mind—escape.

Houdini hated his cage. We tried everything to keep him entertained. We got him a wheel, a plastic ball to roll around in, even these weird chew toys from the pet store. But none of it worked. Every time we turned our backs, that little furball was on the move, squeezing his chubby body through the smallest of cracks and making a break for freedom.

At first, it was kind of funny. We'd find him hiding behind the old washing machine in the basement, his tiny nose twitching as if to say, "You'll never catch me!" Jess would squeal, laughing as we chased him around, trying to scoop him up. But after the third or fourth escape, it got old. The thrill of the hunt wore off when you were trying to drag a hamster out from behind a pile of dusty, forgotten boxes.

Then came the day Houdini pulled his final stunt. Somehow—don't ask me how—the little guy found a way into the furnace ducts. I guess he figured it was the ultimate escape route, but it was also his last. We heard him scurrying around up there for days, trying to find a way out. My brothers even tried to lure him out with sunflower seeds and peanut butter, poking at the ducts with a broomstick, but it was no use. Eventually, the scurrying stopped. And that's when the real nightmare began.

Every time the furnace kicked on, the whole house filled with the smell of burning fur. It was a stench that clung to everything—our clothes, the curtains, even the food we ate. No matter how many windows we opened or air fresheners we sprayed, we couldn't escape it. Jess was devastated. She spent days in mourning, convinced it was her fault that Houdini had met such a grim fate. Meanwhile, I couldn't help but feel a little guilty, too. After all, we'd named him after the greatest escape artist of all time. Maybe if we'd picked a more fitting name, he wouldn't have tried so hard to break free.

The furnace reeked for years. Every winter, the smell would come back to haunt us, a grim reminder of the time we let a hamster take his final adventure through the heating ducts. The memory stayed with us, and some of our childhood dreams officially died with that hamster, as we both moved on.

Jess had become the undisputed queen bee of her little clique they called the Nifty Nine at Holy Ghost. She was the ringleader of her group of giggling, gossiping girls who roamed the halls like they owned the place. Holy Ghost was the Catholic school we attended, and no, it wasn't haunted (though some of the nuns could be pretty terrifying). The name was literal—after the Holy Trinity, of course. But as a kid, it felt strange that my school was named after something as vague and ethereal as a ghost. Jesus might have technically been a ghost after the resurrection, but it still didn't sit right with me. Holy Spirit would've made way more sense!

From kindergarten to eighth grade, I played the part of the good little Catholic schoolboy, repenting from my sinful daydreams and schemes—at least outwardly. My uniform was always pristine: navy slacks, white or light blue polos, with my dirty blonde curls gelled to absolute perfection, thanks to L.A. Looks gel. Every strand was frozen in place, shining under the fluorescent lights of our classrooms. I looked like I had it all together, but beneath that polished exterior, I was scheming a new plan. My goal this time? Not to win a million dollars. No, I had a new goal: I was gonna be famous. No more ripping off old people on the paper route. No more scavenging for Monopoly pieces. I had my sights set higher— way higher.

After school, I practiced guitar religiously, convinced it was my ticket to stardom. I started taking lessons in the church rectory, of all places. The warm red brick of the church stood tall against the sky, its spire reaching heavenward, while the rectory next door exuded a quieter charm. Stained glass windows glimmered softly in the afternoon light, casting patches of vivid color across the walls and floors inside. The air was thick with the unmistakable scent of incense, mingling with the faint musk of old wood and worn hymnals. It was a space steeped in reverence, a strange yet oddly fitting backdrop for a teenage rock star in the making. Something about strumming away on a guitar, dreaming of sold-out stadiums, while surrounded by crucifixes and rosary beads had a certain irony to it. It was like I was both atoning for my sins and setting myself up to commit a thousand more as a rock star.

Everyone in Iowa had a deep love for country music. Rosanne Cash, in particular, was my idol. There was something about her voice that spoke to me, something that resonated with a kid who spent most of his time pretending to be perfect. I must've played her song about that cabaret in a small Texas border town a hundred times: "In a little cabaret, in a small Texas border town, sat a boy and his guitar and people came from all around... and all the girls, from nine to ninety, were snapping fingers, tapping toes, and begging him don't stop." It was my anthem.

Rosanne Cash became my hero. Her songs were my refuge. I sang that same tune in music class, in church talent shows, in front of whoever would listen, like it was the only song I knew. Even when junior high hit and the boys turned sour, and the girls became wicked in their own subtle ways, I clung to that dream. It was the one constant in a world where everything was shifting under my feet.

Junior high was where things went south. The shift was subtle at first, but soon it was undeniable: I was different, and everyone could see it. And in junior high, being different wasn't just noticed, it was punished. The boys grew meaner, the teasing sharper, the jokes more biting. The girls, who had once been innocent playmates, now had a nasty gleam in their eyes. It was like a switch had been flipped, and suddenly, I was the odd one out. My L.A. Looks gel and country music dreams couldn't shield me from the harsh reality that I wasn't like everyone else.

But I didn't know why. Not yet. All I knew was that being different was the worst thing you could be, and I was becoming more of it by the day. I felt like if anyone ever looked close enough, the image I was desperately trying to project would shatter. So, I kept my head down—that became my way of coping. Avoidance. But it wasn't much of a shield. I did my schoolwork, plucked away on my guitar, and quietly existed.

My childhood dreams of million-dollar schemes had faded, but not entirely. I wasn't done trying to game the system—I mean, once you've tasted that sugar-coated delusion of the '80s, it's hard to quit. They promised us a million dollars, dangled it in front of us like candy, and we were hooked for life.

With that in mind, I was ready to be the next Sam Harris, who just won Ed McMahon's *Star Search*. And in my mind, there was no better way to get there than by mastering the guitar. I even thought working at McDonald's could be my ticket to fame—because of course, a Hollywood producer would discover me while I served him up some fries and a quarter pounder and cast me in a national Mickey D's commercial. I practiced filling out fake McDonald's job applications, even though I wasn't old enough to work yet. My plans were big, and I was sure that was the real game in town.

I had a great guitar teacher—this country music singer who lived outside of town in Holy Cross. She was my personal Dolly Parton, with the kind of big, blonde hair that seemed to touch the heavens. Every Thursday after school, we'd meet in the church rectory, and she'd teach me everything from strumming techniques to country classics. Those lessons were the highlight of my week, my escape from the grind of school and the teasing that seemed to be getting worse with every year.

You see, by the time junior high hit, I wasn't just a kid with schemes—I was a target. And I didn't know why yet, but the other boys sure did. Most of the friends I had were adults who felt for me—like my guitar teacher. She was kind, patient, and encouraged me when everyone else was tearing me down.

And then, there was the jacket. My Hollywood jacket. I got it airbrushed at Kennedy Mall that summer—white denim with the word Hollywood splashed across the back in bright neon, like a beacon for my future. It was the jacket I knew I'd be wearing when Ed McMahon saw me and said, "That kid is going to be a star."

But junior high has a way of bringing you back to the real world.

I remember one day, we were on a class field trip, crammed into the back of a school van. We were headed to a farm outside of town to pick apples and learn how to raise pigs, but my mind was elsewhere, dreaming of bright lights and big cities. Bonnie Raitt's "Let's Give Them Something to Talk About" was playing softly from the front seat, and without even realizing it, I started humming along. I knew every word.

And then it happened—the laughter.

At first, it was a snicker, quiet and under the radar. Then it spread like wildfire. The boys in the back were whispering, mocking me in their best falsettos. "Let's give Luke something to talk about!" one of them sang, and the others chimed in, screeching like a choir of laughing hyenas.

I felt my cheeks burn and pulled my beloved jacket tighter around me as we walked into the school. It was like my armor had failed me. The one thing that made me feel powerful now made me stand out like a neon sign for them to attack. My heart sank. I was standing there in the middle of the hall, mortified, while the whole class gathered around to see what was going on. As my head sank into the popped collar of my white jean jacket I tried to hide, I didn't know what to do. Like every little gay kid in America, struggling with this oppression, for some unknown reason, instinctively, we all knew it would get better if we kept our collective heads down. So I started trucking forward, trying to ignore them.

But junior high boys are relentless.

For weeks, their mocking followed me through the halls. I couldn't go anywhere without hearing someone sing that damn Bonnie Raitt song. "Let's give Luke something to talk about!" they'd howl, as I slunk past, my shoulders hunched beneath the weight of their taunts. It was my new reality.

And yet, I didn't stop dreaming. Every Thursday, I still went to my guitar lessons. I still practiced in my room, imagining myself onstage, playing that Rosanne Cash song I loved so much. The boys could sing all they wanted; I wasn't going to stop. But I realized one thing—junior high wasn't going to be about winning. It was about surviving. Yet the constant dings in my veneer were starting to break me.

I'd grown up playing the system, looking for ways to bend the rules in my favor, but in junior high, there were no rules to bend. You either blended in, or you got chewed up and spit out. And me? I was never going to blend in.

That day changed everything. I always left my guitar outside the rectory door on Thursdays. It was too big and clunky to drag around to all my classes, so I stashed it there with everyone else's instruments. It was Holy Ghost, after all. Nobody stole anything here. And Thursdays—they were sacred to me. The one day I could leave the chaos of junior high behind and focus on something bigger, something that felt like me. I would walk down that hall like I was stepping into another world—one where I was on the path to something greater. *Star Search*, Broadway, maybe even fame. It was just a few guitar lessons away.

But that Thursday wasn't like the others. As I made my way to the rectory, the usual excitement I felt started to falter. Something was off. There was this smell—something sour, sharp, lingering in the air. I figured it was the bathroom down the hall; it always had this stench. But as I walked closer to my guitar case, it hit me full force. The smell wasn't coming from the bathroom.

I stopped in my tracks, my stomach knotting with unease. Kneeling down, I flipped open the latches of my guitar case, hoping the smell was something in the hallway. But the moment the case opened, I knew. My breath hitched. The inside was wet—soaked, actually—and the smell of urine hit me hard, making my eyes sting. I sat there, staring, slack-jawed, trying to make sense of it.

They had pissed on my guitar.

It didn't register at first. How? Why? But then it all clicked into place. The guys who had been mocking me for weeks, for singing that Bonnie Raitt song—they had done this. This was their plan all along. They'd been following me, watching my routine, and waiting for the perfect moment. And everyone in my grade knew about it. Everyone but me.

I stood there frozen, my stomach twisting, the humiliation creeping up my neck. What was I supposed to do? I felt gutted. Numb. I closed the case as carefully as I could, even though my hands were shaking. I couldn't face guitar class that day, couldn't face anyone. So I ran. I ran all the way home with that piss-soaked guitar slung over my shoulder, the smell clinging to me, the weight of the humiliation dragging me down.

I ran up the street, took the shortcut through the rocky path, and up the long hill we used to bike as kids. The whole time, my mind raced. I was desperate to make it go away. I couldn't tell my parents. I didn't want them to know. Not about this. So, when I got home, I went straight to the basement—the cold cement floor where we used to chase the hamster. I threw the guitar down next to the drain, grabbed the hose, and yanked it off the wall next to the washing machine.

I scrubbed. I scrubbed so hard that my fingers ached, using everything I could find—Tide, soap, bleach—anything to get the piss out. I didn't care if it ruined the wood; I needed that smell to go away. My tears mixed with the water, dripping into the drain, as I scrubbed until my arms gave out. It felt like I was scrubbing away more than just the piss. I was scrubbing away the shame, the anger, the hopelessness. But no matter how hard I worked, the smell stayed. It clung to the guitar, to my hands, to the air around me. It was like I couldn't escape it.

When I finally gave up, I dragged the guitar up to the attic, threw it into a corner, and locked it away where no one could find it. The attic was always warm and sunny, filled with dust and quiet, and nobody ever went up there. It was the perfect hiding place for something I wished didn't exist. But even as I slammed the attic door shut, the smell followed me. It followed me all the way to my bedroom, where I locked myself in and pounded my head against the door, wishing it would all just disappear.

I couldn't disappear, though. Not really. Despite everything, I still went to guitar lessons. Week after week, I brought that ruined guitar with me. It still reeked, though maybe not as strongly. My teacher never said a word about it. Maybe she didn't notice. Maybe she didn't care. But I knew something had changed. She could see it in me—the way my spirit had cracked. The music didn't sound the same anymore. It was like I couldn't hear it over the screaming in my head, over the lingering stench that haunted me, like that ghost in the attic, kind of like the damn hamster we could smell for eternity.

And even though everything had changed, I couldn't just quit. I knew how much my parents had spent on that guitar, and I didn't want to be the kid who let their hard-earned money go to waste. We didn't have much, and I couldn't bring myself to tell them what happened. Also, deep down, I didn't want them to see how broken I felt. Admitting it would make it real, and that wasn't something I could face. So, I kept going through the motions—strumming the strings, singing the same old songs—because I didn't know what else to do.

But I wasn't the same. The joy I once felt had seeped out of me, replaced by a knot of anger and shame that tightened every time I touched it. The calluses on my fingertips hardened, burning the stench into my skin. It wasn't just an instrument anymore—it was a constant reminder of everything I wanted to escape but couldn't.

After eighth grade, though, I stopped playing altogether. That guitar is probably still up in the attic, rotting away in the heat. It still smells like piss—at least, it does in my mind. But I never talked about it again. It was like it had never happened, though it haunted me all the same, like a curse.

Despite everything that had happened in junior high—the bullying, the shattered dreams, the endless taunts—I made it through. I graduated from Holy Ghost with my head held high, determined not to let those years define me. When I got to high school, I found a new love: the piano. I remember my older sister Heidi always filling the house with Mozart and Beethoven. Jess and I would dance around the dining room listening to her. It wasn't the guitar, but it was an escape, and soon enough, I was really good at it. From the memories of Heidi's recitals, I taught myself Beethoven's "Für Elise," plunking away at the keys in the school auditorium, my fingers flying across the grand piano in the corner of the stage. It became my sanctuary, a place where I could disappear for a while, letting the music wash over me.

High school wasn't easy. The building itself felt like a fortress designed to keep hope out—a brutalist maze of cold concrete and narrow hallways. The skinny windows barely let in any sunlight, casting a pale, lifeless glow on the scuffed gray floors. The walls were thin, wood-paneled partitions separating classrooms from the corridors, with small glass panels at the top to let in light, though it always seemed more like a trickle than a flood. Every sound carried—whispers, laughter, taunts—echoing endlessly in the tunnels of those corridors. Even though I had survived the cruel taunts of junior high, I knew that fitting in wasn't something that came naturally to me.

But the music department was different. Tucked away from the chaos of the rest of the school, it was like stepping into a different world. The rehearsal rooms had soundproof walls, their doors heavy and solid, where I could shut myself away and let the noise of the hallways melt into silence. Surrounded by sheet music and the muted sounds of others practicing, I found something I desperately needed: a place to breathe, a moment of peace, and a chance to lose myself in melodies that made everything else feel a little less overwhelming.

By sophomore year, I had spent two years honing my skills in the music department, and there was a new goal in my sights: the school musical. The buzz in the halls was all about *Grease*. Everyone was talking about it, and I knew I had to be a part of it. My older siblings could recite the entire soundtrack, but I'd never even seen the movie. That didn't stop me, though. I convinced my mom to drive me to Blockbuster, where I snagged one of the last VHS copies on the shelf. I must have watched it a hundred times, memorizing every song, every line, every moment. I knew, deep in my gut, that this was my shot. Becoming a T-Bird was going to be my destiny.

The week of auditions, I walked the halls with *Grease* lyrics running through my head. The tile floors beneath my feet felt like the steps of a stage, and I could practically see my name in lights. When audition day finally came, I was ready. Standing on that creaky wooden stage in the school auditorium, the smell of old velvet curtains filling the air, I belted out "Summer Lovin'" with everything I had. But then, the choir director threw a curveball. He introduced a song I had never heard before, something called "Those Magic Changes." My heart skipped a beat. The play had different songs from the movie, and I was caught off guard. Sweat beaded on my forehead as I tried to remain calm. Luckily, all those years of guitar lessons had taught me how to pick up a melody quickly, and I dove into the song like it was second nature.

The role I was auditioning for was "Doody," a guitar-playing high school kid who dreams of becoming a rock star—a role I was born to play. His big moment happened on the school steps, where his daydreams transported him into a rock concert. It was as if someone had written this part just for me. I could feel the excitement bubbling inside, pushing me forward, telling me this was it. The callback list was posted the next day, and sure enough, I was in the running for Doody against one other guy, Christian—a cute blond kid, like me, who was a year younger. The competition was going to be tight, but I needed this win. After years of letdowns, I practiced that song every single day in the tiny rehearsal closets outside the band hall, humming it under my breath as I walked through the halls.

The day of the callbacks, I stood on that stage again, the familiar creak of the floorboards beneath my feet. The auditorium, with its rows of worn, red velvet seats and the dim light filtering through the high windows, felt like a different world. The director, sitting at the old upright piano, peered at me over the music stand.

"You ready?" he asked. I nodded, gripping the microphone tightly as the first chord rang out. My throat was dry, but I cleared it and sang the opening verse, a bit shaky at first. Then something magical happened. The audience—my classmates, peers who had seen me struggle—began to clap along. The energy in the room shifted, and I felt it flow through me, lifting me up. With every clap, I sang louder, stronger, until by the time I hit the chorus, I was belting it out, my voice soaring above the stage. The girls in the front row were cheering, and for a brief moment, I was transported to another world.

When the callback ended, I knew I had given it my all. The next day, I approached the call board with shaky hands, heart pounding in my chest. I scanned the list, and there it was—my name, next to the role of Doody. I had done it. My classmates congratulated me, it felt like I was on top of the world.

The show was a massive hit. Every night, the auditorium was packed, the lights blazing down on us as we performed. My family sat in the audience, their faces glowing with pride, and I could see my mom wiping away tears when I took my bow. The choreography for "Those Magic Changes" was electric. The girls in the choir surrounded me on stage, screaming and clapping like I was Elvis himself, and I played along, basking in the adoration. For those few nights, I was no longer the awkward kid trying to survive high school. I was a T-Bird, a rock star, and it was glorious.

That stage, that moment, was everything I had dreamed of, and more. It wasn't *Star Search*, but for once in my life, it felt like I had won.

Chapter 3
16 going on 17

But, as is often the case with dreams, the real world has a way of settling in, filling the cracks with something a little more mundane and far less magical. Just like Doody, my fleeting moment as the lead in the high school musical faded, and I was quickly pulled back into the drudgery of everyday life. My days of basking in the spotlight were replaced by cafeteria lines and homework I could barely bring myself to do. The applause that had once echoed through the auditorium was now nothing but a distant memory.

The halls of the school, which once buzzed with excitement after the musical, soon became a gauntlet of whispers and sidelong glances. The football team, maybe a little envious of my time in the spotlight—or maybe just plain cruel—decided to turn my high school dream into a nightmare. It started innocuously enough: a few sneers, a couple of chuckles as I passed by. But then, like wildfire, the rumors spread, fed by the whispers and stares that followed me down every hallway. The school was suddenly abuzz with the story of my supposed "incident" in the boys' locker room—something about me getting a boner in the shower, a story as ridiculous as it was mortifying.

The once-familiar halls now felt like a battleground, and I was the enemy on every side. I tried to brush it off, sulking down the hallways with my eyes glued to the floor, but the damage had already been done. The football team had made sure of that. My "celebrity status" had been reduced to whispers behind cupped hands, rumors that stung worse than any cheap locker room insult. And although it was completely untrue, in high school, it didn't matter if it was real or not—it mattered that people believed it.

I'll never forget the day in choir when my friend pulled me aside and, with a look of pity, whispered, "You know what they're saying about you, right?" I could feel my face go hot as the blood rushed to my cheeks. I didn't want to hear it, but there was no avoiding it. The rumor had taken on a life of its own. I was the talk of the hallways for all the wrong reasons. From that day forward, gym class became a strategic mission to avoid the boys' locker room. If I couldn't skip gym entirely, I'd hide in the bathroom stalls to change, doing my best to blend into the tiles and pretend like I wasn't there. That would be my routine for the next three years.

But the truth was, the rumors, the taunts, the relentless mockery weren't new. They had been circling me like vultures since that incident with the guitar back in junior high. I had been marked as different long before I ever knew what that even meant. The slurs that followed me down the hall—homo, queer—were as common as the books I carried to class. And the football team? They were especially cruel, the ringleaders of a misery circus that had no off-season. They'd wait until my mom was parked outside the school gates to pick me up, and they'd scream "fag" as I opened the door. It was miserable. I hated them; and I was starting to hate myself.

One day, as I entered my history class, a brief wave of relief washed over me. The classroom, with its scuffed floors and faded posters of ancient civilizations, felt like a refuge from the chaos of the hallway. Here, in the far corner of the next-to-last row, I could momentarily escape the snickers and side-glances that haunted me elsewhere. Mr. Potterman, the varsity football coach who doubled as our history teacher, was already at his desk. Short, stocky, and with a booming voice, he commanded the room with an authority that didn't come from textbooks but from the sidelines. He wasn't a fan of teaching, and it showed. His gaze drifted more often toward the star players in the class than to the crinkled pages of history he was supposed to be guiding us through.

I slouched down into my seat, placing my books on my desk as a barrier between me and the rest of the room. I'd already read through today's assignment—something about China's role in World War II—but I wasn't really paying attention. I was looking for some mental cover. History was supposed to be about wars far removed from my world, but it felt like every day was a battle just getting through the school day.

As students trickled in, the air thickened with the usual chatter and jostling. Half the football team filled the desks around me, their booming voices and muscular frames dominating the space. Among them was Jared Bradfield, the poster boy for every high school crush. His golden hair glowed in the classroom's hazy sunlight, and his blue eyes always seemed to be laughing at something. Girls wanted him, guys wanted to be him, and here I was—wanting to disappear in front of him.

The jocks sat in their usual spots, the noise rising in volume as they told inside jokes and recounted their latest locker room antics. I tried to ignore them, keeping my head buried in the textbook while my fingers absentmindedly tapped a rhythm on the desk. It wasn't much, but it was my little escape from the swirl of taunts and jeers. Jared sat behind me, the heat of his presence palpable as my back stiffened against the chair.

"Hey," a voice whispered, too close to be anyone else but Jared.

My heart jumped. What the hell? Jared Bradfield never talked to me. My brain scrambled for a response, but before I could even turn around, he whispered again, his breath warm against my ear. "Wait for me after class."

What did that even mean? My pulse raced, and confusion clouded my thoughts. Was this real? It couldn't be. I knew better than to believe the golden boy of the football team would seek me out for anything other than a laugh. I spent the rest of class trapped between dread and ridiculous excitement, barely registering Mr. Potterman's lecture on post-war geopolitics. Was it a joke? I could already feel the pit of anxiety gnawing at my stomach.

The bell rang, a sharp jolt that signaled the end of class. My palms were clammy as I slowly gathered my things, trying to delay the inevitable. As the room cleared out, Jared was still there, standing by the last row of desks with that confident grin that could charm anyone. I swallowed hard, forcing myself to breathe.

I made my way toward the door, but Jared blocked my path, his arm casually resting against the desk, preventing any easy escape. "Hey," he said again, that low voice sending shivers down my spine. "I was thinking... maybe you and I could hang out sometime?"

What the— This wasn't happening. My brain couldn't process what Jared was saying. Was this for real? I stood there, dumbfounded, clutching my books like they were some kind of shield.

"Uh... like... hang out? Why?" My voice wavered, and I could hear the panic rising. This had to be a joke. But before I could say anything else, Jared leaned in closer, his smile broadening, and whispered, "You've got beautiful eyes."

And that's when I knew. The heat that flooded my cheeks wasn't from embarrassment—it was the flush of realization. This was a setup. It had to be. I instinctively glanced toward the door, and sure enough, a few of the other football players were standing there, barely containing their laughter.

Without thinking, I tried to push past Jared, but he moved his arm, blocking me again. "What's wrong? You don't wanna go out with me?"

I was paralyzed between fury and humiliation. My throat tightened as I tried to move around him, but Jared followed, his voice dripping with mock sincerity. "I mean, come on, Luke... we'd be perfect together."

※　The door creaked open as the hallway erupted in laughter. I broke free, bolting down the hall as fast as I could. Their laughter echoed in my ears, sharp and searing, as Jared's parting words trailed behind me: "Luke! Let's give 'em something to talk about."

By the time I reached my locker, my hands were trembling too much to turn the dial on the lock. The hallway was still buzzing with chatter, but all I could hear was the sound of those boys laughing, their voices trailing behind me like a haunting refrain. The damage was done. I could feel their eyes on me, like vultures circling overhead, waiting for the next moment to swoop in for the kill.

SLAM! My locker door crashed shut, inches from my face, and there was Chad Steel, the homecoming king—broad, smirking, and ready to twist the knife. "What's up, dork?" His voice dripped with condescension, and I could feel the eyes of the hallway on me, watching, waiting for the show.

For a moment, I wanted to disappear. To be invisible. But I knew I couldn't. Not anymore. The hall fell silent for a split second, long enough for the tension to break. Without waiting for his response, I turned my back and walked away, leaving behind the whispers and the laughter, but carrying the weight of it all with me.

"Um, dude. Um. Leave me alone," I stammered.

"You got somewhere to be?"

"Yes, I have English. Can I pass?"

"Not so fast, fag. I hear you think you're too good to go out with Jared?"

"Um, no. Um, what are you talking about?"

Chad towered over me and yelled for all the students to hear, as if quoting some stupid rabbit from a cereal commercial "Silly faggot, dicks are for chicks!" As he picked me up and slammed into the back of the lockers, and punched me. Pain rippled through my body. I fell to the floor.

Next thing I knew, I was in the nurse's office, the harsh fluorescent lights hummed overhead, stinging my eyes as I squinted against the brightness. My body ached all over, and I winced as I felt a sharp pain spreading across my rib cage. The sterile smell of antiseptic filled the small room, mixing with the faint scent of old, worn bandages and paper towels. It all felt surreal, like I was floating outside of my body, hovering over the aftermath of the beating.

The nurse, a kind but weary woman who had probably seen her share of bloody noses and bruised egos, hovered nearby, her eyes scanning my face for signs of something deeper than physical pain. She didn't ask questions, just quietly handed me an ice pack wrapped in a thin towel, gesturing for me to press it against my face. Her silence was both a comfort and a burden. I didn't have to explain, but the weight of what happened felt heavier for being unspoken.

Then, she cleared her throat. "Luke," she said softly, "the principal wants to see you."

My stomach twisted into knots. Of course, the rumors had made their way up the ladder, crawling like a sickness through the school hallways, infecting every corner. I couldn't take it anymore—the whispers, the accusations, the endless barrage of lies. I wasn't sure what would be worse: facing the principal or going back out there to face my classmates.

The nurse led me down the hall, her soft shoes squeaking against the polished floors, while I tried to steady my breathing. The walk felt endless, each step echoing in my head, the oppressive weight of the school's walls closing in around me. Posters about school spirit and anti-bullying campaigns lined the hall, their messages bitterly ironic.

When we arrived, the principal's office door loomed in front of me, as if it were a portal to another kind of punishment. The nurse gave me a small, sympathetic nod before she opened the door and gently nudged me inside. The room was cramped and stuffy, with the sharp scent of freshly brewed coffee masking the mustiness of old books and papers piled high on the principal's desk. He sat there, hands folded, his expression unreadable, but I could feel the tension radiating from him like heat off a fire. His dark suit jacket looked a size too big for his frame, giving him the appearance of someone who had been shrunk by years of administrative burden. He motioned for me to sit.

"I've heard some disturbing rumors, Luke," he began, his voice flat, not accusing but not sympathetic either. It was just a statement of fact, as if I were some kind of case file rather than a person. "There are stories going around, about things happening in the locker room, and... I want to give you the chance to explain." As if I was the one who had something to apologize for!?

The words felt like lead in my chest, heavy and suffocating. I couldn't breathe. My heart raced, but my mind felt sluggish, as if my body was preparing for a fight but my brain refused to follow. Was the principal of the school asking me about my erection?! Jesus, did the entire staff know? What was I supposed to say? What could I say? That the football team had singled me out, harassed me for years, and beaten me up because of some made-up rumor? That they had concocted this lie to make me out to be something I wasn't?

I opened my mouth, but no words came out. I couldn't tell the truth. If I did, I knew what would happen. I'd get branded as a tattletale, and that would just ramp up everything I had already endured. The football team ran this school. If I exposed them, there'd be hell to pay.

"I—" I stammered, but the words caught in my throat. My hands trembled in my lap, the ice pack from the nurse now forgotten. "I don't know what you're talking about."

The principal's eyes narrowed. He could tell I was lying, or at least not telling the full truth, but he didn't press me. "Luke, if something's happening, you can tell me. We can take care of it."

I shook my head. "Nothing happened," I said, the lie burning in my throat. "It's just rumors. They're not true."

He sighed, a heavy, tired sound, and sat back in his chair. "All right," he said, though his tone suggested he didn't believe me. "But if you ever feel like you need to talk about it, my door is open."

I nodded mechanically, mumbling a quick "thank you" before bolting out of the office as fast as I could. The hallway stretched out in front of me like quicksand, each step heavier than the last. I felt like I was sinking deeper and deeper, no way out, no way to breathe. My head pounded, my heart ached, and all I wanted was to escape. I couldn't face them again—the football team, the jocks, the stares, the whispers. I had to keep my head down. Keep moving forward. That's all I could do.

So I trudged through high school, each day feeling like walking through a never-ending fog. Every class, every hallway encounter felt harder than the last. I started taking different routes, ducking into empty classrooms or slipping out of side doors to avoid the guys who hurled insults and threats my way. But through it all, one dream kept me going like a distant beacon: leaving this town.

Heidi, my big sister, had gotten out and gone to college, and I knew that was my only way out too. Even my mom, during those years, started studying for her own college exams, determined to do more than just bake cakes. She was transitioning from Susie Homemaker to Rosie the Riveter, proving not only to herself but to us as well that there was more out there for women to achieve. It wasn't just about getting a degree—it was about reclaiming a sense of purpose. Heidi was a catalyst for that, and I'd watch them pour over financial aid forms together late at night, figuring out federal loans to make it possible.

Those years were tough. My mom worked all day at the bakery and went to classes all night. My dad took over the cooking, and our dinners became a predictable rotation of chicken or spaghetti. Jess and I would laugh on the walk home, trying to guess which one it would be tonight. But we missed my mom's pot roasts. It was hard watching her come home from class at 8 p.m., exhausted, only to sit down in her chair and start studying. Sometimes she'd fall asleep right there, her notes still in her lap, before we even went to bed.

Her determination became my lifeline. College wasn't just a vague aspiration—it was my one chance to escape this small-minded place and breathe freely for the first time. My grades were mediocre, and my SAT scores weren't much better, but I didn't care. I wasn't aiming to become a scholar. I just wanted to become something more, to step into a world bigger than this town.

College wasn't exactly within easy reach for me, though. My undiagnosed dyslexia was a constant hurdle, one that no one seemed to notice or understand. At the time, I didn't even know what to call it. Words danced around the page, letters swapped places, and sentences blurred into a tangled mess. While other kids breezed through their homework, I'd be stuck rereading the same sentence, battling to make sense of it all.

Teachers, despite their good intentions, chalked it up to carelessness or lack of effort. I was always told to "try harder" or "focus more," as if I wasn't already working overtime just to keep up. The other kids sped ahead, leaving me in the dust, while I fought to untangle the letters and numbers that always seemed to slip away.

I learned to compensate in my own ways—memorizing where I could, skimming through dense material, and using my creativity to fill in the gaps. But those whispers of "not living up to my potential" haunted me. So, when I thought about college, it felt like a mountain too steep to climb.

How could I make it when I was barely scraping by here? College demanded good grades and high test scores, and if those failed, I'd have to get serious about acting. That was my only other shot at something bigger—bigger than the small town, bigger than the shadows of the rumors that followed me. I had endured high school's battlefield and survived, but I wasn't leaving without taking my shot at the big leagues. The dream of becoming a star kept me moving forward, even as those rumors grew louder and the words on the page fought me at every turn.

My town boasted a well-respected community theater. During high school summers, I'd participated in a few shows, always finding solace on that stage. But this year, something bigger was on the horizon: a paid Summer Stock Theatre program was launching for the first time, with their inaugural production being *The Sound of Music*. Not only was it professional theater, but they were offering real money—$500 a week for the leads. This wasn't just any opportunity; this was the break I'd been waiting for. After all, I had my sights set on Broadway, and what better way to get there than by stepping into the shoes of Friedrich Von Trapp?

Confident from my show-stopping performance in *Grease*, I walked into that audition with my head high and my heart full. My heartfelt rendition of *Edelweiss* practically felt like a promise. I could feel the room respond, as if it were mine for the taking. And sure enough, a week later, when the cast list went up, my name was right there next to Friedrich. I had done it! Not only that, but my little sister Jess, who had tagged along to auditions, was cast as one of the Von Trapp children too. We looked the part as siblings, and everything felt perfectly aligned. It felt like I was on cloud nine, the whole world finally recognizing the future star I knew I was.

With graduation around the corner, it seemed like the stars were finally lining up. *The Sound of Music* was the perfect launchpad, and Broadway didn't feel so far off anymore—at least, not in my daydreams. I could almost see the stage lights, hear the applause, and feel the weight of my name in lights. The future was there, waiting for me to step into it.

But dreams have a way of crashing into reality, don't they?

While I was floating on the high of landing the role, those long-awaited college letters began to trickle in. One by one, they delivered nothing but disappointment. Rejection after rejection piled up in my hands, each letter a reminder that my mediocre C average and extracurricular achievements weren't enough to catch the admissions boards' attention. My heart sank a little more with each letter, and the bright future I envisioned began to dim.

When I thought all hope was lost, I received one final envelope. It was from the state university, the one Heidi and her best friend Jill had attended—the one that had always been my top choice. I tore it open with shaking hands, bracing myself for another blow. But instead, the first words I saw read: "Congratulations! You've been accepted to Iowa State University..." My heart leaped... until I read the rest: "...on a preliminary basis."

Preliminary? What did that even mean?

As it turned out, I wasn't fully accepted. There was a catch—one that felt more like a trap. I had to complete two summer courses and achieve a B average before I could be granted full admission in the fall. A B average was already a stretch for me, especially with my struggles in school. And to make matters worse, the summer program was in a town four hours away.

That's when it hit me: I was facing an impossible choice.

On one hand, I had *The Sound of Music*, the dream role, a professional gig that would pay me $500 a week. It was everything I had worked for, everything I had dreamed of—a foot in the door to a life in theater. On the other hand, I had college—the one chance I had to escape this small town, to become something bigger than the life I'd known. But I couldn't have both.

The decision was agonizing. How could I choose between the future I saw on stage and the one that could come from a college degree? One offered immediate gratification—an actual paid acting role. The other offered the potential for a different kind of future, one with stability and possibilities beyond what I could imagine in my small-town bubble. I felt torn in half, my heart pulling me one way, my head pulling me the other.

In the end, the decision made itself. As much as it broke my heart, I had to turn down the role of Friedrich. College was my way out, my chance to build something bigger than this town, and if I didn't go now, I might never get out. While my friends, and Jess, would be on stage living out my dream that summer, I would be stuck in a sweltering classroom, paying for all those years of poor test scores in high school. My dreams of Broadway were on hold, replaced by textbooks and a desperate hope that I could pull off the grades I needed to stay in school.

As if to twist the knife further, Christian—the same guy who had been my competition for the role of Doody back in *Grease*—was cast in my place as Friedrich. He had become a friend after the show, and while I was happy for him, it stung to see him step into the role that was supposed to be mine.

Still, I knew this was what I had to do. Dreams, after all, aren't always about the spotlight. Sometimes they're about sacrifice. And maybe, just maybe, I could make my way back to the stage after I had climbed this mountain called college.

Summer school was nothing like I had imagined. Instead of the fresh start I'd hoped for, it proved to be an isolating and exhausting experience. With student housing closed for the summer, I found myself living alone in a sparsely furnished apartment—if you could even call it that. The walls were bare, the furniture reduced to the basics: a bed, a small desk, and a chair that wobbled every time I shifted my weight. The quiet hum of the refrigerator was my only companion most nights. It wasn't the bustling college life I had pictured; it was a far cry from the stage lights of *The Sound of Music* or the camaraderie I had once hoped for. College, as I soon learned, was an intimidating new landscape, and I felt adrift, unsure how to navigate this strange, adult world or how to make real connections with my classmates. One night, roaming the aisles of Walmart, trying to pass the time, I ended up in the party aisle buying rolls and rolls of colorful crepe paper streamers, and I decked that drab little apartment out like it was my birthday all summer.

But still, the loneliness gnawed at me, and the evenings were empty. To escape the isolation, I sought out familiar comforts. The local mall became my refuge—a place to wander aimlessly, where I could disappear into the aisles of Waldenbooks, flip through records at Musicland, or lose myself in the flashing lights and constant chatter of the arcade. The mall was a far cry from the theater, but at least it was somewhere I could feel something—a bit of that old buzz of life and interaction I craved.

Out of sheer desperation for social interaction, I applied for jobs at all three stores. I needed something—anything—to fill the time and the silence. A few days later, I landed a gig at the arcade, where

I would stand behind the counter, doling out quarters to kids eager to spend their afternoons lost in *Street Fighter* or *Mortal Kombat*. It wasn't glamorous, but it kept me busy, and the noise of the machines and the energy of the kids made the loneliness a little more bearable.

Most nights, the arcade would quiet down after 8 PM. That's when I would pull out my sociology and English homework, laying it across the counter as I worked under the dull glow of fluorescent lights. The hum of the machines and the faint sound of coins clinking in slots became the backdrop to my determined effort to maintain those elusive B grades. I couldn't afford to fail—not after giving up *The Sound of Music*. The stakes felt higher than ever, and I poured every ounce of energy I had into passing those classes.

By the end of summer, I had done it. I scraped by with B's in both courses, securing my spot for the fall semester. That victory, though, was still bittersweet. I finished just in time to make it back home to see *The Sound of Music*. Sitting in the audience as my friends—Jess included—belted out songs on stage was gut-wrenching. I should have been up there with them, basking in the spotlight, but instead, I'd traded it for summer school—a choice that lingered in the back of my mind like a weight I couldn't quite shake. But as I left the auditorium, I reminded myself of what truly mattered. As Maria said when she finally left the abbey, *'When God closes a door, He opens a window.'* I'd made it into the fall semester, and I was staring out that window.

Before I left for college, my mom and I sat down around her cherry-colored countertops. "Luke," she began, her tone soft but serious, "you've got so much talent. I've spent my life watching you paint rainbows, frosting cookies, scribbling out your stories in colored pencil. I see what a storyteller you are. Every time you take the stage, I know you feel so much joy. But you need something that'll pay the bills, too. Something like marketing or graphic design—it's just another yellow brick road you can follow, and maybe it'll lead to a real job. Follow your heart, do the school plays too, but…" She trailed off, her eyes searching mine, as if hoping I'd see her wisdom before she had to spell it out.

I didn't want to admit it, but she was right. Her practicality always had a way of grounding me, even when I didn't want to be grounded. As much as I hated the idea of choosing something "practical," I knew deep down that she wasn't trying to stifle me— she was trying to protect me. By the end of the night, after hashing it out over my final admission papers for the fall semester, graphic design was officially my declared major.

Looking back, I realize that choosing something stable wasn't just about survival; it was about honoring the effort my mom had poured into giving us opportunities she never had. Still, as much as I embraced the practicality, my heart would always belong to the stage. That was a dream I wasn't ready to give up—not then, not ever.

College, as it turned out, was a different world. Gone were the cruel rumors and taunts from high school; here, people didn't seem to care about my past—they actually seemed to like me. I quickly formed friendships with the theater majors, who were as quirky and driven as I was. So I split my time across campus. But before long, I landed a spot in the chorus of the school musical, *Bye Bye Birdie*. The atmosphere backstage was electric, and I finally felt like I truly belonged somewhere. I even smoked my first cigarette behind the theater with a few castmates, feeling rebellious and grown-up as the smoke curled around us in the cool night air. It was thrilling, and slowly, I began to find my footing in this new world.

But, as with all good things, the semester came to an end far too soon. I was back at home, standing in the same high school bedroom I had grown up in. The walls were still the same faded sponge-painted blue, and the familiar smell of hamster wafted up from the air ducts—stale, burnt fur that I could never quite forget. It was a sharp reminder of where I was and how far I still had to go. My college life, with its vibrant friendships and theater performances, felt like a distant dream. Back here, it was as if none of that had happened.

I managed to find work waiting tables at Chi-Chi's, a local chain Mexican restaurant popular with families and teens. My nights were spent refilling soda glasses and clearing plates of enchiladas, while the tips were barely enough to fill the gas tank. Yet, it was something to do, and it pulled me out of the house.

In between shifts, I fell back into old habits—cruising up and down the strip with my high school friends, hanging out at the video store for hours, watching movies we'd seen a hundred times already. We'd drive around, aimless but content in that way only teenagers can be, the glow of the streetlights passing by in a blur. It was comfortable, familiar, but it didn't feel right anymore. That small-town rhythm I had once known so well now felt suffocating, like I was slipping backward. The promise of something bigger, something grander that I had felt during the school year seemed to slip further and further away with each lap we took around town.

College had changed me in ways I hadn't expected. It had shown me what life could be like beyond the walls of this place, and as much as I loved my friends and my family, I knew I couldn't stay here forever. My escape plan was still intact, but that summer back home reminded me how narrow the window to that future really was. The next semester couldn't come soon enough.

That summer, the weekends began to feel like an escape—not only from the rigorous nights at Chi-Chi's but from the stifling routine of small-town life. One particular weekend, a group of us ventured out into the wilderness, hoping to reconnect with nature—or at least, that's what we told ourselves. It was supposed to be a "man's trip," the kind that teenage boys take to prove they're becoming men. I was usually surrounded by girls, which felt safe and familiar, but this summer had been different. Most of the girls were away, and I had found myself bonding with a new group—a more male-dominated crowd.

This wasn't the football team, who had spent most of high school making my life hell. No, these were the A-wingers, the music department guys who spent more time with sheet music than weight training. This was my tribe: me, Christian—who had taken my role in *The Sound of Music*—his twin brother, and a few guys from the marching band. We were an odd mix, but it worked.

That weekend, we drove two hours out of town to some camping grounds, where we pitched our tents in the shade of towering evergreen trees, with plans for a weekend of canoeing, hiking, and campfires. The air was thick with the heat of a typical Iowa summer—ninety degrees by noon, the kind of heat that sticks to your skin and makes you feel like you're melting. Sweat dripped down our necks as we set up camp, but we laughed through it, thrilled to be free from parents and responsibilities for a few days.

By Saturday, a bunch of the guys had decided to go fishing at the lake. Fishing, of all things. I wasn't interested in fishing—I wasn't exactly the "put a worm on a hook and wait" type. I mumbled something about being tired and said, "No, I'll hang back." Christian, to my relief, also had no interest in fishing. He stayed behind too, and we spent the afternoon lounging near the tents, soaking up the sun and talking about nothing in particular. Christian was easy to be around, with his laid-back attitude and sharp sense of humor. We had bonded over music, theater, and now this newfound sense of freedom.

But the whole time, I was caught in a battle I didn't quite understand—my Catholic values, my upbringing, and the simple fact that I was a teenage boy with raging hormones, surrounded by a group of half-naked, bare chested guys. I tried to push the thoughts aside, forcing myself to ignore where my eyes kept wandering. But it wasn't easy. There was something simmering beneath the surface, and I didn't know how to handle it.

Eventually, after hours of pretending I wasn't distracted by the sight of Christian lying shirtless next to me, I made an excuse. "I'm gonna take a nap," I said, gesturing to the tent. It was an escape, really. Somewhere I could hide from my own confusion, shut out the noise in my head.

I crawled into the tent, the small space quickly becoming stifling from the summer heat. I stretched out on one of the sleeping bags, willing my mind to quiet down, but moments later, Christian followed. He plopped down onto a sleeping bag next to me, and the air felt even thicker, hotter, more tense. We were cramped in the small tent, lying side by side, and though we were both pretending to nap, I could feel the space between us shrinking. The sounds of the lake and the distant laughter of our friends faded, leaving only the hum of our shallow breaths in the close air.

I closed my eyes, willing myself to sleep, but it was impossible to focus. My heart pounded in my chest, not from heat exhaustion, but from something deeper. I could feel the tension between us, the way the air seemed charged with an energy neither of us knew how to address.

Then, without warning, Boom!

Our legs brushed, a small, almost imperceptible touch, but it sent a shockwave through me. I could feel the heat radiating off his skin, the air inside the tent was too thick, too hot to breathe. Christian shifted next to me, and for a split second, I thought—no, hoped—that he felt it too. That maybe, just maybe, I wasn't alone in this confusing mess of emotions.

I lay still, pretending to be asleep, but my mind was racing. This wasn't about friendship anymore. Something was changing, something I didn't fully understand yet, but I could feel it. And in that moment, I knew this wasn't the last time I'd have to confront these feelings.

And I can't remember if I turned over or if Christian turned over—but suddenly, BOOM! He was kissing me. It felt like a thousand fireworks going off inside of me. BOOM. BOOM. BOOM. Just like in that old Brady Bunch episode where Bobby finds love and everything goes up in cartoon hearts and explosions. It may have been ninety degrees outside, but in that tent, it was 110.

My heart was racing, my mind spinning, but it wasn't fear anymore—it was something else. The kind of rush that you feel in your bones, in your fingertips, in every nerve firing off like it had been waiting for this very moment. I was kissing a guy. And even though that thought had never fully formed before, in that instant, it felt like the most natural thing in the world. Like this was what my body had been waiting for.

The world outside the tent disappeared. Everything—the trees, the lake, the whole damn summer—it all fell away as the only thing that mattered was the heat of his skin, the way our breath tangled together, the frantic rhythm of our hearts pounding in the thick, sweaty air of that cramped, rough canvas tent. BOOM. BOOM. BOOM.

It was crazy. It was terrifying. And yet, it was the most right thing I'd ever felt. My body, my brain, every single part of me was shaking, unraveling, coming apart at the seams. I was experiencing sensations I didn't even know existed, let alone that I could feel with someone else. It was like everything I had been holding back, all the confusion, all the buried feelings, were unleashed, spilling out uncontrollably. And from the way Christian's body was reacting, I knew he was feeling it too.

Separated, we both lay back, catching our breath, shirtless, staring up at the glowing cloth roof of the tent, our bodies still trembling from what had just happened. That's when it hit me—this was my awakening.

For the rest of the weekend, Christian and I were inseparable. We became masters of sneaking off. "Hey, we're going over to the picnic table to look at the stars," we'd say to the others. A casual excuse, but we both knew where we were really going—into the shadows of the evergreens, where we'd crash into each other, pulling off shirts, unbuttoning denim jean shorts, and losing ourselves in that intense, electric connection. BOOM.

It was like a drug. The rush, the thrill, the secrecy—it felt so good, so addictive. And every time we found a hidden corner of the camp, it was like we grew bolder, more in tune with each other, our bodies becoming more familiar, more comfortable in this new territory. Each kiss lasted longer than the last, each touch more confident, and as the summer days melted together, so did we. BOOM, BOOM, BOOM.

Afterward, lying back, catching our breath, pine needles crunching under our weight, Christian turned to me, a smirk playing on his lips.

"Do you think they know?" he whispered, his voice still shaky from the rush.

I laughed, nervously, turning to meet his gaze. "Oh my god. No! You think? No one said anything. Do you think it's obvious?" I blushed, I could feel my cheeks turning red.

He paused for a moment, his eyes flicking back to the stars. "Does this... I mean, does this feel real to you?" His voice had softened, a vulnerability creeping in that hadn't been there before. I swallowed, unsure how to answer. "More real than anything else," I finally said, my voice barely above a whisper.

He smiled, a sad kind of smile. "Yeah... same. It's like nothing else matters when we're out here. Like everything disappears."

We lay there in silence for a moment, the weight of unspoken words hanging in the air. Our connection still echoing, but now softened by something deeper. Something neither of us were ready to admit.

We left the next morning, drove home, the hum of the highway filling the spaces between us, and for a few heated weeks in August, Christian and I kept the magic alive. Late nights turned into secretive parking lots, hidden cornfields, and moments stolen in the dark. It felt like the entire world had shrunk to just the two of us, with only the sweltering Iowa summer keeping time.

As the days grew shorter and the air began to change, a quiet understanding settled between us—this couldn't last; I didn't live here anymore. But we desperately tried to outrun it, chasing the sun as it dipped lower in the sky, pretending we could hold on to that enchantment a little longer. But like all summers, this one had to come to an end. And with it, so did the spell we'd been under.

As August turned into September, my high school friends and I started getting ready to return to college for the fall semester. The familiar classrooms, the hometown streets—they were all places I no longer belonged to. With a heavy heart, I packed up my things for college. I left behind the summer of stolen moments, of Christian, of first kisses, of that first taste of freedom—and I returned to a life I could barely remember, a life that now felt far less exciting, far less real than the one I had just lived.

Lost in the haze of longing for Christian, I sought solace in the university's theater department. My heart was still tangled up in memories of those secret summer nights, the heat of our whispered confessions and stolen moments lingering long after they ended. I thought of him every day—his golden hair, his easy smile, the way we fit together like a secret we never wanted to share with the world. But he was far away, back in high school, a life that now felt like a distant memory I couldn't return to.

Six weeks into the semester, during an audition, I was unexpectedly captivated by someone new. He was magnetic—a corn-fed Iowa boy with an air of innocence that bordered on angelic. He had that wholesome, farm-boy charm that seemed to make everyone in the theater department fall head over heels, girls and boys alike. He was like a prince out of a Disney movie, and soon, the theater was thick with drama. The lines between fantasy and reality blurred. I was drawn to him, caught between the pull of this new infatuation and the ghost of Christian, whose shadow still loomed large over my heart.

By the time Christmas rolled around, my emotions were a tangled mess. The crush on this new boy had become all-consuming, and my heart was a chaotic battleground. One night, drunk off half a bottle of peach schnapps at a holiday party, I found him in a dark corner, making moves on a girl. It felt like a punch to the gut. The booze and jealousy ignited something wild inside me, and before I knew it, I had confessed my feelings to him, laying my heart bare for everyone to see. The fallout was swift and messy. We were both confused, conflicted about our sexualities, and my emotional outburst didn't win me any points. Instead, I was spiraling out of control, turning my love into something unrecognizable. Years of being bullied, of hiding feelings I didn't understand, of feeling excitement for the first time and the sting of rejection—it all boiled over.My friends saw the mess I was becoming. After I put my fist through a window, leaving me bloodied and shaken, they knew it was serious. They pulled me aside, calmed me down, and, without my knowing, called my family back home. Terrified for me, they felt they had to let them know what was happening. At one o'clock in the morning, my parents and little sister, Jess, huddled around the phone, trying to make sense of the distressing news pouring in from Iowa State, unsure how to help—me or my friends. I sat buried in my room, alone with my thoughts and the icy realization of what I'd done.

In the weeks that followed, I found myself scribbling sad poems on concrete walls, spiraling down like a tortured French poet, full of heartbreak I couldn't seem to shake. The weight of it all was suffocating—Christian, the new boy, the confusion of my own desires. I was lost.

Heartache clung to me like a shadow. I wasn't sure how to feel about Christian anymore, even though a part of me knew he still loved me. But now in my own pain, I was hurting people around me. During Christmas break, my mother sat me down for a conversation I didn't expect. She told me that my roommate had called her, telling her everything about my mental state, and they mentioned a boy over the phone. The news stunned me. "What did they say?" I asked, bracing for her response. I was terrified of what she might know, and what she might say next.

She looked at me and said, "We've known for a long time, since you were young. We have, and always will, love you for everything you are." Her words were calm and direct, and they cracked open a small space for understanding. The fear I'd carried for so long started to shift, but it didn't disappear. It clung to me, even as I tried to untangle the impossible standards I'd built around myself.

Could I ever make peace with any of it? The harm others inflict on you and the harm you inflict on yourself—they're two different battles, and after all this time, I'm still fighting mine. That much is obvious, given how personal I've been up to this point and how quickly I'm moving through one of the most difficult parts of my life. I'm sorry—I'd like to give you more than that, but... Being gay is who I am—I wear it on my sleeve, even back then when I didn't want to. The word just couldn't define who I felt I was—and it didn't need to.

The heartbreak and rejection felt like it was shattering my entire world, leaving me with pieces I didn't know how to put back together. It would take years to figure it out. My mom, who had put her college education to use working as a counselor at the hospital's drug and alcohol rehabilitation center, suggested I attend a 12-step program there during the rest of my break. It wasn't because I had a problem, but because she believed the therapy and steps might help me gain perspective. Desperate for a way to cope, I agreed. Sitting in those meetings, I searched for something—anything—that might help me find peace. When I returned to school, I joined group therapy, still hoping to discover what I needed to finally accept myself.

Christian and I met a few times after Christmas, but life was moving faster than we could keep up with. His senior year was coming to a close, and he had plans to leave for California, chasing dreams we'd once whispered about during our summer nights. When spring break came, we shared a bittersweet kiss, knowing it would likely be the last. We said our goodbyes, and though I didn't know it then, that was the final chapter of us. I never saw him again in person...

How To Win a Million Dollars

For anyone out there struggling, if you, like me, have ever felt beaten down and left with nowhere else to turn, please know that there is always someone who understands. Throughout my life, I've faced moments where I wanted to harm myself. If you ever find yourself in that place, please reach out to The Trevor Project. You can call **1-866-488-7386** or text "**678678**" for help 24/7. There are people who can listen, help, and care for you in a dark moment.

Please know you are not alone.

Chapter 4
It's Urine, not You're In

Now, it was my junior year of college, and I don't know if you partied like it was 1999 in 1999, but let me tell you, it wasn't exactly the carefree celebration Prince promised. It was more of a goddamn fear fest. Y2K loomed like some biblical disaster, and the whole world was teetering on the edge of a full-blown technological apocalypse. Surges of fear rippled through my body as the clock ticked down the hours to midnight.

I couldn't concentrate on anything except the thought of satellites falling from the sky, planes nosediving into the earth, and the power grid collapsing—all at once. For weeks, the news had been blaring about this disaster, claiming that anything with a clock, a computer chip, or a single digit in its system would just... stop. And there wasn't a damn thing anyone could do about it. I sat there at a basement party, thinking, *Jesus Christ, of all the things engineers could've planned for when building their army of world-dominating electronics, how did they all collectively forget to program the computers to handle the year 2000?* I mean, really? We had thousands of the smartest people in the world, and not one of them thought, *Hey, maybe the calendar should know what comes after 1999?*

The night was shaping up to be a full-blown catastrophe! People everywhere were stocking up on canned goods, water, and flashlights, preparing their bunkers for the end of civilization. Meanwhile, here I was, home for Christmas break, sitting in a random high-school basement with no bunker, no emergency food stash, and absolutely no plan beyond hoping I'd survive the night.

To be fair, the basement was probably one of the safer places to be when the clock struck midnight—at least I wasn't standing out in the open waiting for a satellite to drop on my head. But still, there was no escaping the fear. It was all anyone could talk about, and as if my nerves weren't already shot from finals and existential dread, now I was trying to accept the fact that I might die in 30 minutes, with all of my dreams of getting rich and famous flushed down the toilet! So, I did the only sensible thing I could think of: I gathered up my wits, grabbed a couple of girlfriends, and huddled in the corner with a vodka cranberry, biting my nails and trying not to hyperventilate.

The minutes dragged on like a slow-motion car crash. Every second felt like it lasted a year. My hands were clammy, and I was sweating through my Abercrombie & Fitch t-shirt. The countdown started—10, 9, 8—and I was bracing for the worst. *Planes are going to drop out of the sky,* I thought. *Satellites are going to crash through the roof, power grids will fry, and all of us will be vaporized in a split second.*

5, 4, 3, 2, 1... *HAPPY NEW YEAR!!*

The lights went out with a pop! Total darkness. The entire basement plunged into an inky black void.

People screamed. I screamed. There was panic, total chaos. I stood frozen, clutching my drink like it was the last lifeline on earth. *This is it. This is really it.* They weren't lying. *Every single computer on the planet has shut down. We're done.* My mind raced. *How far are we from the airport? Was this a terrible spot to party? What the hell were we thinking?*

I was preparing for certain death, eyes darting around, trying to find a doorway to stand under, like that was going to save me from the apocalyptic fall of civilization. I was practically shaking. *This is it. This is how I die. Right here in this basement with these idiots.* And then—POP! The lights came back on. Everyone screamed, but this time, it was in pure relief.

Except my friends? They were doubled over, shrieking with laughter. Turns out, they'd been the masterminds behind the blackout. "Gotcha!" they roared, grinning like Cheshire cats. They had flipped the circuit breakers at midnight to mess with all of us who were on the verge of cardiac arrest.

I stood there, still in a state of shock, before muttering something about needing another drink. I poured myself a stiff second vodka cranberry and let out a shaky laugh. Crisis averted. The world was still spinning, and Y2K had turned out to be nothing more than the prank of the century—or at least, the prank of the night.

With the Y2K madness behind me and winter break winding down, I returned to college ready to tackle the second semester and, hopefully, find a new job that didn't involve quarters jammed in arcade machines or cleaning up after hyperactive kids at birthday parties. Sure, the arcade had been fun for a while—dishing out cheap prizes and wiping up spilled soda while keeping an eye on the Street Fighter games—but let's be honest, I wasn't going to graduate college with my biggest achievement being my ability to disassemble a video game console to release a stuck quarter.

I needed something new, something creative. Something that spoke to the artist in me. So, one day, after coming home to an empty fridge and deciding to take on the daunting task of grocery shopping at Econofoods, the chain where my mom use to decorate cakes, fate intervened.

There it was, like a neon sign on a dark highway: the Floral Shoppe (yes, with the extra "pe" at the end, as if it were striving for "more than this provincial life!") right inside the grocery store. And what did I spot at the counter? A big, glorious "Help Wanted" sign. Ding ding ding! This was my moment. My calling. I'd always had a flair for aesthetics, after all, and flowers were basically nature's artwork, right? So following in my mothers footsteps, I imagined myself decorating, but this time in elaborate bouquets, arranging roses like a pro, and maybe even getting discovered for my impeccable taste in floral design.

I grabbed the application, chatted up the cashier girls at the counter (flirting a little too much in hindsight), and within a week, I had the job. I was officially a floral shoppe employee—no, superstar! I was about to become the best bouquet designer this side of the Des Moines River, or so I thought.

The real world, however, had other plans.

As a fresh hire, the reality of my job wasn't the glamorous, creative floral design role I had envisioned. Nope. Most of my shifts were spent scraping the thorns off long-stemmed roses and stripping leaves from pre-made $5 bouquets that flooded the shop day after day. Those cheap bouquets? They were probably our best sellers— big buckets of carnations, daisies, and baby's breath that I had to refill every night as they sold like hotcakes.

The real custom bouquets? The fancy FTD orders I imagined myself crafting like a floral Picasso? Well, almost no one ever ordered those. Most days, I didn't even step into the walk-in cooler where we kept them. Instead, it was all about filling buckets with water, snipping stems, and keeping the $5 bouquets looking somewhat fresh for the crowd of hurried grocery shoppers.

And then there was the waste. You wouldn't believe how many flowers we tossed in the garbage. As soon as the stems began to rot or the petals wilted just a bit too much, into the trash they went. I couldn't help but feel a little pang of guilt with each bucket I filled with discarded blooms. After a while, I realized how wasteful this whole process was. These flowers weren't dead-dead; they still had a few days of life left in them. So, I did the only sensible thing: I took them home.

Now, technically, I didn't think of it as stealing—it was more like rescuing. I mean, these flowers were going to the trash anyway! It was practically a public service. Senior citizens had probably picked over the bouquets, and if I didn't bring them home, they'd just be gone forever. So, night after night, I loaded up with slightly wilting daisies, limp carnations, and half-dead roses. My apartment quickly became a jungle of dying flowers, and on any given day, only half of them were in various stages of decay. But hey, it's the thought that counts, right?

Spring arrived, and with it came a new wave of products: potted plants! They came in by the truckload. And you know what happened next? The staff, who didn't have a green thumb among them, started overwatering them, drowning the poor things until they were soggy, wilting messes. More plants went into the trash. I took them home too. Soon, my apartment wasn't just filled with dying flowers—it was a full-blown greenhouse, potted plants spilling out of every corner. If anyone walked into my place, they might've thought I was starting a floral rescue mission.

I'm pretty sure the statute of limitations on "stealing" almost-dead plants and flowers has passed, so I feel comfortable sharing that now. But back then, I had a personal jungle going, and it was all thanks to my job at the Econofoods floral shoppe.

Most of my shifts were in the evening, when foot traffic in the floral section slowed to a trickle. So, I'd bring my schoolbooks, plop down behind the counter, and get to work on my classes. I wasn't a model student by any means, but I was scraping by. And while I was supposed to be learning sociology or cramming for some English exam, my mind was always elsewhere: daydreaming of Broadway, of New York City, of a life that didn't involve $5 grocery store bouquets.

I had built up quite the collection of Broadway CDs over the years, thanks to those CD clubs that promised ten free albums if you bought ten more within the year. I must've signed up, canceled, and re-signed a dozen times. I mean, I had every show album from *Annie Get Your Gun* to *Xanadu*, but little did I know, my obsession with filling my CD collection was driving me deeper into credit card debt, swipe, cha-ching! Budgeting wasn't exactly my strong suit, but hey, Broadway dreams don't come cheap.

And as I sat there in the floral shoppe, surrounded by roses that were more dead than alive, I knew one thing for sure: I wasn't going to spend the rest of my life arranging grocery store bouquets. I had bigger dreams, and no matter how many plants I "rescued," I was going to find a way out.

Back at the flower shop, I had a ritual. Every night at 8 o'clock sharp, I knew that the Broadway curtains were rising in New York City. While I was stuck in Iowa, I tried to be a part of that magic from afar. So, every night at exactly 8 PM, I'd press play on my cast recording of *Footloose*. For the next hour or so, the floral department would transform into my very own Broadway stage. I wasn't stacking buckets of flowers or stripping thorns from roses anymore—I was Ren McCormack, the rebellious city kid trapped in a town where dancing was banned. I sang every note, nailed every harmony, and in my head, the bouquets became my audience, clapping wildly after each number.

The story of *Footloose* revolved around a preacher's son who died in a car accident. The preacher then convinces the town to ban dancing—a move that set the stage for rebellion. Enter Ren, a rebel outsider determined to shake things up. Played by Kevin Bacon in the movie, Ren was everything I dreamed of being. For a kid like me, stuck in a small town with big dreams, that role wasn't just a character—it was a symbol of everything I wanted to be. I could practically hear the roar of applause as I belted out "Almost Paradise" to the refrigerated cases of carnations and daisies. Every word, every song, every night, I practiced like I was preparing for the biggest audition of my life. My one dream was to leave Iowa behind, get to New York, and actually audition for *Footloose*. I was convinced that was my ticket out.

Fast forward to the end of my senior year—I did it! I graduated with a BA in graphic design and, thanks to piling up so many extracurricular theater credits, I ended up with a minor in performing arts too. My parents were ecstatic, just like getting out of the factory early, they saw a future for me too. Diploma in hand, I had plans. I wasn't exactly rolling in cash, but I did have $300 to my name. So, I packed up and moved to Staten Island, of all places, with a couple of college friends from the theater department. They had a tiny extra room they were willing to rent for $150 a month. It sounds like a dream now, but in the early 2000s, yes, you could actually live in (almost) New York for that price!

I decorated my little room—a glorified closet on the third floor of a dilapidated brown bungalow—with the budget of a starving artist. A $10 can of paint from the hardware store and a handful of dollar-store trinkets turned my space into something magical. Sure, there wasn't much room to move, but in my mind, it was my very own slice of the Big Apple. The house didn't have a living room, just three bedrooms and a whole lot of creaking floors. And while my "magical" room was affordable, it was also on Staten Island, which meant commuting was a nightmare. I had to take the bus to the ferry, then hop on the subway to make it all the way to Times Square. The whole trip took about an hour and a half—each way. But none of that mattered. I was in New York.

Although, it was imperative to find work, or I'd end up back in Iowa. The small-town boy with big dreams had a short runway, scraping by on a few hundred dollars a month and a credit card (swipe, cha-ching). Staten Island wasn't exactly the glamorous New York I had imagined, but I could afford it. I told myself that I was just like Madonna. She moved to New York with nothing but her dream, a few hundred dollars, and an attitude ready to conquer the city.

Except, instead of being a bright-eyed hero with a lucky break, I found myself one night staring out the window with my roommates—peak excitement on Staten Island. Out of nowhere, we watched a guy emerge from the bushes, yank a driver out of his car, and steal the vehicle right in front of us. We stood there, mouths hanging open, and that's when it hit me—I needed to start "movin' on up" as quickly as possible.

My friend from college, Kim, who had played Reno Sweeney in our production of *Anything Goes*, was tall, thin, with long brown hair that seemed to go on for days. But even she only had it slightly better than me when she moved to New York a year before I did. She had landed an apartment in Hell's Kitchen, blocks from Times Square, but her living situation wasn't exactly glamorous either. She shared a one-bedroom apartment, which meant sleeping on the couch while our other college buddy claimed the bedroom. Their apartment, to make matters worse, was positioned directly beneath the Port Authority bus terminal. All night long, buses rumbled past her window, shaking the walls and making it nearly impossible to sleep. And if that wasn't enough, there was a fish market right on the corner. Every morning, the workers would toss buckets of putrid fish water onto the street, filling the block with the unmistakable stench of rotting fish. Hell's Kitchen was certainly living up to its name.

Despite the less-than-ideal conditions, Kim had one major advantage: she was working for a real Broadway production company. She had landed a job on the marketing team at Dodger Theatricals—the same company producing *Footloose: The Musical* on Broadway. Yes, the *Footloose* I'd been singing along to in the flower shop. Kim's job involved creating flyers and posters, going to state fairs on Long Island to perform songs live with a karaoke setup, and promoting the show to the world. It was my dream job! When I finally made the leap to New York, I joined Kim at Dodger Theatricals in what was essentially an unpaid internship. My role? Following people around, and hoping someone would notice I could be useful. I loved it!

Our office was in the heart of it all, 1501 Broadway, right across the street from the TRL (Total Request Live) studio at MTV. Outside, Times Square buzzed with an energy that felt almost electric. The streets were alive with a constant flow of tourists, street performers, and honking taxis, all illuminated by a kaleidoscope of neon lights and flashing billboards. Giant Broadway posters towered above us, some as tall as three-story buildings, advertising the latest shows with larger-than-life stars beaming down. A steaming Cup o' Noodles sign perched above the chaos, letting out real clouds of vapor into the crisp city air, like some surreal mascot for the hunger and hustle of New York. But inside our office, the energy shifted from the dazzling spectacle outside to the behind-the-scenes frenzy of Broadway itself. I was learning the ropes in a world just as chaotic and captivating as the streets below.

The Music Man was playing at the time, and since I had been in the show four times back in Iowa—playing every part from Winthrop to Tommy Djilas—I knew the play like the back of my hand. So when Kim's co-worker, the company manager of *The Music Man*, took a liking to me, I jumped at the chance to help him out.

The company manager's job was to manage the logistics between the cast and the producer, making sure everything ran smoothly behind the scenes. He was basically the producer's right hand at the theater, and he handled everything from payroll to actor contracts. I'd follow him around, file checks, and even got to hand them out to the actors after the shows. It was thrilling to be part of the inner workings of Broadway, especially for *The Music Man*—my hometown Iowa's own swan song of a musical. The lyrics couldn't have captured home better: 'Oh, there's nothing halfway about the Iowa way to treat you, when we treat you, which we may not do at all.' It was true: kindness sure wasn't halfway back then—sometimes it felt nonexistent. The show had a way of making a boy realize how far he'd come.

One night, after dinner and a little too much wine (just like Hugo Peabody, I could get drunk off milk), we ended up backstage at the theater. Now, I had been backstage at the show plenty of times before, but this night was special—Peter Gallagher was there, hanging out after seeing the show. The Peter Gallagher! Known for movies like *While You Were Sleeping* and *American Beauty*.

In my tipsy state, I didn't recognize him right away for his movie star status. I knew that face looked really familiar. So, in true Luke fashion, I blurted out, "Hey, dude, I know you from somewhere! Where do I know you from?"

Peter Gallagher, of course, gave me nothing—just a polite smile as I made a fool of myself. My sober self would have instantly recognized him, but instead, I stood there, a 21-year-old intern, tipsy on a Broadway stage, mistaking a Hollywood actor for someone I might've gone to high school with.

Embarrassing as it was, the company manager didn't hold my drunken gaffe against me. He even introduced me to some of the folks working on new shows. It turned out they were looking for someone with experience in web design and coding. Thank God my mom had pushed me to get a graphic design degree! I had spent a whole year honing my skills in web design and coding classes at Iowa State, and I wasn't half bad. I met with the marketing team the next day and they talked to me about creating a website for a quirky off-Broadway show called *Urinetown*. It had originally premiered at the New York Fringe Festival and was now making its way to off-Broadway, soon to be destined for the big time. The next day I was hired! (Always listen to your parents, kids!) The irony wasn't lost on me; the title of my memoir could have easily been, *From Piss Guitar to Urinetown: The Lucas Stoffel Story.*

But in that moment, my Broadway dreams began to take on a new form, expanding beyond the stage and into the business side of theater. Creating the website for the show was my first real step into the world I'd always dreamed of. My skills were rough, but it was more than anyone else could do in the marketing team. Back then, in 2001, the World Wide Web (that's what we called the internet, hence the www in a URL) was still like the Wild Wild West—uncharted and mostly unexplored. Most people didn't really know how to navigate it, let alone build something from scratch. HTML, CSS, even the idea of a website for a Broadway musical was a brand new concept. And here I was, just a kid, already on the cutting edge, knowing how to turn a few lines of code into something people could actually see and interact with online.

It felt amazing to bring *Urinetown* into that digital space, giving it a presence that few theater productions had at the time. This opportunity wasn't just a backstage pass; I was becoming part of something magical. By the time the show opened off-Broadway, I had landed a job backstage, finally getting my foot in the door (or should I say, the bathroom door) of the theater world.

The first day of rehearsals was surreal. I had the script in hand, a cassette tape of the music (yes, cassette tapes were still a thing), and I sat down in the theater, ready to scribble notes as part of the team. The rehearsal room itself was a scene straight out of a Broadway dream: floor-to-ceiling windows flooded the space with natural light, offering a panoramic view of the city skyline. Mirrors stretched across one wall, reflecting the energy of the bustling room back at us, while a circle of white tables sat in the center, scripts piled high, as actors filed in.

And then it hit me—the entire cast of Footloose was there! Jennifer Laura Thompson, Hunter Foster, and other performers I'd idolized from the show were now in front of me, casually flipping through the pages, chatting, and preparing to bring the story to life. My heroes, the people whose voices I had sung along with every night in that floral shoppe, were now part of my life. I was starstruck, and for a moment, I had to remind myself to breathe. This was it— the moment where dreams crossed over into reality, and I was lucky enough to witness it firsthand.

But let me tell you, working off-Broadway wasn't all glitter and lights. After the website was up, I got a job working in the theater. Part of my duties during the run-of-show included turning the air conditioner on and off during the quiet scenes, selling overpriced beer to theatergoers, and, yes, the grand finale—cleaning the toilets once the curtain closed. That's right, I cleaned the toilets at *Urinetown*. Here I was, making $45 a show and scrubbing urinals— but I got to keep the extra cash from the beer sales. My job was literally recycling itself, turning tips into piss. It ended up being not half-bad money.

My parents back in Iowa still had no idea what kind of strange-sounding show their son was involved in, or that he had to scrub out the urinals as part of the gig. They'd call me and ask, "You're working on a show called what? *You're In Town... You're in town for what?*"

Eyebrows raised in confusion. "*Urine*, Mom, *URINE-town*, not 'You're in town!'" I'd say. "Ya know, like, Pee Pee town." They never got it, but I knew we were going places.

The theater itself was something else entirely—housed on the second floor of a functioning police station, the American Theater of Actors felt more like a relic of another era than a polished venue. To reach it, you'd walk past on-duty officers before entering, where a grand spiral staircase awaited. Worn down by time, its once-elegant curves now creaked underfoot. At the center of the staircase stood a circular open-air elevator, permanently stuck between the first and second floors—a ghostly remnant of the building's forgotten past.

At the top of the staircase was a dim, crumbling space with ten rows of dilapidated theater seats. The velvet upholstery was fraying, peeling back to expose the padding beneath. It could barely be called off-Broadway—it was that rough. The space had once been a courtroom, and while the high ceilings and traces of wood-paneled walls hinted at its history, the transformation was stark.

The set designer leaned into the theater's ruggedness, painting the entire stage black and creating a raw, industrial aesthetic. A midnight steel grate balcony was built at the back, resembling a fire escape, and the centerpiece was a tiled subway wall that rolled fluidly across the stage. A movable steel grate staircase connected the balconies in a variety of ways, adding to the dynamic, urban atmosphere. The result was a minimalist yet striking setting.

It was the perfect setup for *Urinetown*, a show set in a dystopian world where people met a grim fate for breaking bathroom laws. Penelope Pennywise ran Public Urinal #9, the play's main setting, and made sure the whole town knew it was a privilege to pee. She'd belt at the locals, "Twenty years, we've had the drought, and our reservoirs have all dried up. I take my baths now in a coffee cup, I boil what's left of it for tea..." she'd sing. Then, in her stern tone, she'd yell over the crowd, "No one gets in for free. Every morning, you all come here. And every morning some of you got reasons why ya ain't gonna pay. And I'm here to tell ya, ya *is* gonna pay!"

If you couldn't pay the toll, if you dared pee on the street, you'd get carted off to *Urinetown* by Officer Lockstock and his Deputy, Barrel. And in Act II, we learn the dark truth—*Urinetown* isn't some far-off place; it's just being thrown off the top of a building. Splat.

But of course, I was in heaven, selling beer in the lobby of the show with my Broadway idols just a few feet away was a dream come true. Then came one of the best nights of my young life. It was my birthday, and I was working a show. Jennifer Laura Thompson— the lead of the show and my hero from *Footloose*—walked in with a birthday cake and began singing "Happy Birthday" to me! The house manager, John Lloyd Young, who would later win a Tony for starring in *Jersey Boys*, was the one who got me the cake, but hearing Jennifer sing was like Marilyn Monroe showing up to serenade me. Only a year ago, I'd been daydreaming in the back of a flower shop; now, my Broadway daydreams were becoming reality.

Six months later, *Urinetown* moved from off-Broadway to the Henry Miller Theatre on Broadway. I wasn't cleaning toilets anymore, thank God, but I had made it to the big leagues. I worked backstage and managed the stage door. Sure, my office was what could only be described as a janitor's closet, but now I was part of Broadway history.

Normally, stage door attendants were unionized, but when the Henry Miller Theatre had been rebuilt after years of hosting *Cabaret*'s Kit Kat Club, the usual rules didn't apply. Only the stage was unionized, which opened up a secret little pocket of Broadway history just for me to slip into.

Standing there at the stage door each night, watching actors rush in and out and handing checks to the stars felt like a far cry from my flower shop days. It felt like this was just the beginning.

I spent most of my days hunched over my laptop in that broom-closet-turned-office. Since the job often had a lot of downtime, I used my ingenuity and design skills to pick up side hustles, building websites for any of the actors who came through the door. It was small and cramped, but I stayed there, learning every nook and cranny of backstage life and soaking up the energy of the theater around me.

That's where I first met Laura von Holt, or as she liked to call herself, "von Hottie." She was a burst of energy in human form—bubbly, rambunctious, with her platinum blonde hair and a mischievous grin that made you feel like you were in on some grand secret. Laura was bustling around the theater world, determined to make it big, just like me. She had an infectious joy that could light up the room and was full of smart, quick-witted comebacks.

Since *Urinetown* was preparing to open on Broadway and Laura was interning at Dodger Theatricals, it was only a matter of time before we collided—like some sort of cosmic bump in the chaotic swirl of Broadway life. Meeting her at the front desk was like stepping into a whirlwind of energy. She was bursting with enthusiasm and always on the move. Laura wasn't just smart; she was prepared. If I needed something—whether it was a pencil, stapler, or even a highlighter—she'd already have it in hand before I could even finish the thought. It was like she had an endless supply of everything, and she whipped around the office getting things done in record time. I remember thinking, *This lady is impressive; she's got it together.*

Laura eventually left her internship to return to school at Sarah Lawrence, and I didn't think much about it at the time—Broadway is filled with people who drift in and out of your life like passing scenes in a play, and it's easy to lose touch. But when 9/11 happened, everything changed. New York felt like it had been cracked open, and all the noise and chaos that usually filled the city went silent. From her college dorm room, Laura emailed me to check if I was okay. With the tragedy hanging over the city, our fleeting summer memories became something more—an anchor in a storm.

That morning had started like any other. The ferry ride to Manhattan was calm, the skyline clear. But in a flash, everything changed. I was on the deck when the first plane hit the World Trade Center—black smoke billowing over the water. I pulled out my Nokia phone, called my mom, and left a message on the answering machine: "Mom, I think something's happening. I'm okay right now." Moments later, the second plane flew over our heads and struck the second tower. The ferry stopped dead in the water, leaving us stranded in the bay near the Statue of Liberty. The explosion was so massive, we could feel the heat on our faces from half a mile away. Time seemed to stop as we watched in horror while the towers burned.

I dialed home again, this time reaching out to my mom's office at the hospital. They transferred the call to the red phone, a direct line reserved for emergencies. She picked up quickly. "Mom, I'm okay, I'm on the ferry..." was all I managed to get out before the line went dead. Around me, the chaos was overwhelming—people were sobbing, frantically trying to reach loved ones. One woman collapsed to the floor, crying out, "My son, my son is on the 81st floor!"

We all stood frozen, unable to look away. Eventually, the ferry docked back on Staten Island, and we rushed onto the pier. People had parked their cars with the doors open and radios blaring, trying to make sense of what was happening. The news was relentless—reports the Pentagon might be hit, hijacked planes, and terror spreading. Then, right before my eyes, the first tower collapsed. Manhattan vanished beneath a cloud of smoke. I bolted up the hill, running as fast as I could, one eye glued to the skyline. I was panicked, desperate to get home and understand what was going on. When the second tower fell, I stopped in my tracks. The cloud of debris engulfed Brooklyn and it seemed like it had vanished too, as if the end of the island had fallen off. The city I passed through every day was crumbling before my eyes.

By the end of the day, Manhattan felt like a war zone. Threats of danger in Times Square, tunnels closed, rumors swirling of terrorists on the loose—it was chaos. All the bridges to Staten Island were shut down due to bomb threats, and we were locked in. They intended to turn the ferry into a makeshift morgue, bringing bodies to the stadium, but no one was ever found in the rubble, and the fires kept burning. Even now, I can still see the smoke in my mind—the towers I walked past every day, gone in an instant. It hardly felt real.

In the end, I was lucky. I had been running late that morning because a Coca-Cola truck had blocked our bus while unloading and made me miss the earlier ferry. Those five minutes kept me out of the disaster zone. The next few days, we went to the shore and stared at the skyline—smoking, broken, and no longer the same.

The opening of *Urinetown* was delayed for several weeks after 9/11, and Broadway went dark. But when the time finally came, I invited Laura to join us for the opening night. Even though she had left her internship, she had helped me all summer, and it felt right to share this moment with her. We dressed up, put on our best faces, and had a small party. It wasn't the jubilant celebration we had envisioned—everything was quieter, more somber—but being together mattered. All the lights on Broadway had been turned off that night to honor the city's grief, and though the world had changed, we were grateful to be there, contributing in whatever way we could. That's how Laura and I stayed friends. Without that shared moment of connection, I probably would have lost touch with the woman who once helped me find pencils and staplers.

By then, I had been working on the show for over a year, and seeing the show rise from its humble beginnings was exhilarating. The critics embraced it, loving the unusual title and its offbeat nature. They even made playful puns: "Don't hold it in! Go see *Urinetown*!" The little Iowa boy inside me couldn't have been prouder to see our quirky show go from an abandoned courtroom theater where I once cleaned toilets and sold beer, to a bona fide Broadway hit. Subway posters and taxi cab signs across the city boasted our logo, announcing us as one of the hottest shows in town.

Even my parents, who were still puzzled by my involvement in a show with such an odd title, traveled all the way from Iowa to see what exactly I was doing in New York. I could tell by their faces they were worried I'd gotten myself into something strange. But when they sat in the theater, saw the packed house, and heard the laughter and applause, they finally started to get it. *Urinetown* wasn't just an oddball show—it was the next chapter in my journey. From our small Midwestern town to the bright lights of Broadway, I had made it. And for me, it was the culmination of years of daydreaming, hustling, and rehearsing in the back of that floral shop, imagining what my life might become.

As spring approached, the air crackled with excitement as the show received an astonishing 10 Tony Award nominations. The energy backstage was electric, every conversation revolving around the upcoming awards. I couldn't believe the journey we had been on—a scrappy show about paying to pee, now standing on the precipice of Broadway's highest honors. The 2002 Tony Awards fell on my 24th birthday, and I knew I had to share this moment with my little sister, Jess. She had never been to New York City before, so her week-long visit was packed with sightseeing and late nights, all leading up to the big event on Sunday, June 3rd.

Jess brought along her floor-length scarlet gown from senior prom, the fabric iridescent under the lights. Her perfectly highlighted chestnut hair was curled and pinned up with delicate jewels, forming a tiny baby's breath halo that sparkled, framing her face like something out of a fairy tale.

"Look at you," I said, nudging her with a grin. "Ready to dazzle the whole crowd."

She rolled her eyes, laughing. "Please, I'm just here for the after-party."

As for me, I rented a sleek, black fitted tuxedo for the occasion. I looked sharp, feeling every bit like we were ready to step into a crowd of paparazzi, the flashbulbs capturing our every move.

It was a surreal moment for both of us, two siblings who had grown up dreaming of something bigger, now walking the red carpet at Radio City Music Hall. Thinking back to our grade school schemes, the very idea that we were here now, rubbing elbows with the biggest names on Broadway, felt like we had achieved a dream.

Inside, the atmosphere was electric. My friend Laura, now out of college and making a name for herself in the theater scene, shimmered as her golden hair cascaded down her back. With sapphire earrings and a diamond-encrusted necklace that could make your eyes pop, she looked radiant in her dark blue gown as she joined us at our seats, looking every bit as if she were here to receive her own award.

Laura gave a playful glance around the theater. "Just think, a few months ago, we were running around finding office supplies to fill up your broom closet. Now look at us!"

"Yeah, now we're mingling with Hollywood royalty," Jess added, feigning a regal wave to a nearby couple. "Are you sure I don't have dirt from the cornfield on me somewhere?"

Together, we skimmed the program, eyes darting nervously across the categories. *Urinetown* was nominated for Best Actor, two

Best Actress nods, Best Featured Actress, Best Choreography, Best Orchestrations, Best Original Score, Best Direction, Best Book, and, of course, the holy grail—Best Musical. The weight of the evening pressed down on us like never before.

As the night unfolded, so did our nerves. Best Actor? Lost. Both Best Actress nods? Lost. Featured Actress and Choreography? Gone. The sinking feeling was almost unbearable. We were holding on to hope, but the reality of losing big seemed to be setting in.

Next, Best Original Score. I leaned forward, clutching Jess's hand. "And the winner is... *Urinetown*!" The words exploded from the stage, and we shot out of our seats in disbelief. A Tony! Our little show had won a Tony Award! We screamed and hugged each other, riding the adrenaline as we barely settled back into our seats. Next up was Best Book. Could lightning strike twice?

"And the award for Best Book of a Musical goes to... *Urinetown*!"

Fireworks. Pure, joyous chaos erupted in Radio City Music Hall. We were two for two! *Urinetown* had now won two Tonys for Best Score and Best Book. Our faith was restored, and our hearts raced. One more, and we could have the big one.

Best Direction was next. The tension in the air was suffocating as the envelope opened. "And the winner is... *Urinetown*!" And then we lost our minds! Jess and I screamed, our director bounded on stage, and the cast erupted in celebration. With three wins under our belt—Score, Book, and Direction—there was only one category left: Best Musical. Could we really pull it off?

The final category arrived: Best Musical. The entire theater seemed to hold its breath, the weight of the moment almost too much to bear. Blythe Danner, radiant under the spotlight, stepped forward with the final envelope of the night. We were teetering on the edge of victory, on the verge of realizing the wildest dreams any of us had dared to imagine.

"And THE WINNER IS..." She paused, the entire room collectively holding its breath. "*Thoroughly Modern Millie!*"

The room seemed to freeze. I could feel the shock ripple through the audience like a wave. Jess and I stared at each other, mouths gaping. *Thoroughly Modern Millie*? What just happened?

It was true that *Millie* had taken home Best Actress and Best Choreography earlier in the night, but it hadn't won any of the major categories that traditionally led up to Best Musical. Our team, after clinching three massive awards, had felt like the inevitable winner. But now, in the blink of an eye, everything was ripped away. Confusion washed over the auditorium. The night that had seemed destined for triumph ended with us standing in disbelief, our hopes dashed.

And now, to have the ultimate million-dollar prize snatched away at the last moment felt like a devastating blow. In an instant, everything was gone. Best Musical, the award that could cement our place in Broadway history, slipped through our fingers as if it had never been there at all. It was as though the rug had been yanked from under our feet, and we were left stumbling, grasping for something—anything—to hold on to.

The shock, the confusion, the disbelief hung in the air like a thick fog. How had this happened? We had done everything right, every box had been ticked, and yet... we'd lost. What earlier had almost felt like it belonged to us was ripped away in a single breath.

We sat there, stunned. Hearts racing. Minds spinning. So close. So painfully, devastatingly close.

Chapter 5
The Starving Artist

In the back of the Broadway theater, tucked away in a tiny broom closet with three Tony wins under our belt, I'd felt almost famous for a while. But as year four of working backstage rolled around, the edges of my Broadway dream began to fray. Sure, the thrill of being part of something monumental still lingered, but the day-to-day routine was wearing thin. I'd switched to the day shift—when the show wasn't performing—because someone had to keep things running smoothly: signing for packages, checking in with the wig and laundry crew. Most days, I had more downtime than tasks, spending about 50% of my time in the quiet, dimly lit corners of the theater, left to my own thoughts.

Though the show had been a success, the broom closet wasn't bringing me fame or fortune. And I was starting to wonder: Was this really it? After years backstage, the dystopian world of Urinetown started to feel less like satire and more like a grim mirror. The show's story was built on Malthus's doomsday predictions—who argued that, in the near future, there'd be too many people, not enough resources, and, well, a lot of death. Cheerful, right? Basically, he painted a world where we'd all end up fighting over a drop of water while choking down some bourgeoisie's version of dehydrated birthday cake. Night after night, the goofy, dark musical made the audience laugh—then squirm—as it asked whether striving for more would lead to anything other than a spectacular, literal nosedive into collapse.

It struck a nerve. I had spent so much of my life scheming for ways to get ahead, chasing money like it was the golden ticket in a Willy Wonka sweepstakes. But watching *Urinetown* unfold on stage night after night, I couldn't help but wonder: Was I stuck in the same capitalist dance routine, chasing freedom while the only real reward was disillusionment? Every time the cast belted out *Run, Freedom, Run,* I couldn't help but feel the irony. Sure, the show made me clap along, but it also left me thinking, Well, crap. Now what?

So I started looking for something new. In those quiet hours backstage, I decided to fill my downtime with a new quest—a quest for knowledge, or at least something to keep my mind busy. So, naturally, I tried to learn French. How does a dyslexic who spent most of his life wrestling with English even think about tackling French? Well, in the most dyslexic way possible—by skipping the formal lessons that had failed me before and diving straight into what worked. I watched movies dubbed in French with English subtitles—*The Little Mermaid, Beauty and the Beast,* and every Disney movie I could get my hands on. It wasn't traditional, but something about the rhythm clicked. Oddly enough, this casual immersion taught me more than the three years I'd spent stumbling through French class in high school, where words on a page always seemed to trip me up. Here, I could hear the language, see the patterns, and it began to make sense.

I had been obsessed with Paris for as long as I could remember. As a kid delivering newspapers to elderly neighbors and scouring the streets for millions, I was captivated by Heidi's best friend, Jill—a kid from Iowa, just like me. With heels in her bag, fire in her soul, and her signature siren-red hair, Jill had moved to France, gotten married in a castle, and had two kids. Her story lodged itself in my brain like a song on repeat. If she could live a fairytale in Paris, why couldn't I?

And so, with every dubbed French movie and every dream of Parisian streets, I was preparing myself for the next chapter. My time in New York was winding down. Broadway had happened, but now I was ready for something new. I spent hours at Crate & Barrel on Houston and Broadway, staring at an Eiffel Tower print, picturing my life beneath its arches. Paris wasn't a daydream anymore—it had become my next goal. I had gone from wanting to walk down streets of gold to dreaming about finding a humble hovel in Paris, to become like one of the greats—Oscar Wilde, Baudelaire, Van Gogh, or Picasso—somewhere I could dive deep into my burning artistic passions!

The idea of leaving it all behind started as a whisper, a fleeting thought that grew louder each day. The City of Lights called to me like a siren, promising adventure and a chance to reignite my passion. As winter turned to spring in *Urinetown,* I had finally squirreled away enough money, bought a ticket, found an apartment, and paid in full for the summer, with an extra seven hundred euros of spending money in my pocket. I was getting ready to go. I wasn't fully prepared, but I had signed up for French classes.

The prospect of uprooting my life was nerve-wracking. My savings were minimal—barely enough to scrape by—and my grasp of French was laughable. What if I failed? Doubt gnawed at my excitement, but a flicker of determination pushed me forward. I needed to take this leap. But first, maybe, I could convince my partner in crime, my little sister Jess, to join me. As the phone rang in Iowa, I could almost picture her face—the confusion melting into a wary smile as she picked up.

"So, what do you think about spending the summer in Paris?" I blurted out before she could even say hello.

"Paris? Luke, are you serious?" Her voice was half-laugh, half-shock, but I knew I had her interest.

"Yes, Paris!" She hesitated, and I seized the moment. "You've got the whole summer off from school, and I've got a plan. We'll figure it out as we go—I've already rented a place to stay. We'll be just fine."

"Think about it—do you really want to spend the summer back in Dubuque? I mean, I know there's a lot of glitz and glamor at the Kennedy Mall, but..."

"Oh, very funny," she teased, but I could hear her curiosity stirring.

"Remember, we used to be kids who had adventures!" I said. "And if a French explorer could end up the founder of a tiny town in Iowa, then two kids from the cornfields can definitely carve out our own adventures in Paris."

A long pause hung in the air. Then finally, a sigh. "Luke, you're crazy, you know that?"

"But crazy enough for Paris?" I pressed, grinning into the phone.

She laughed, and I could almost see her shake her head in that way she does.

A few days later, I received a text: "All right, let's do it. Paris."

Next thing we knew, we had landed at Charles de Gaulle on a bright, sunny afternoon—the kind of day that makes you feel like anything is possible. I had a loose grasp of how to navigate from the airport to the heart of the city, which I diligently planned out on MapQuest and printed. With a sense of adventure, I took Jess by the hand, and we hopped on a train, setting off on a journey through a maze of train switches and underground tunnels that eventually spit us out in the Marais. Its tiny streets twisted and curved, guiding us toward the heart of the neighborhood.

Our apartment was about ten blocks north of the Pompidou Center, so we followed our crinkled paper map, tracing our steps to Place de la République. There, we found Rue de Nazareth—an inconspicuous little street filled with wholesale clothing shops, a hairdresser's, and a butcher. It wasn't the picture-perfect Paris from postcards, but it had its own charm, and that was good enough for me.

We approached a small steel gate with a tiny blue plaque that read "32 Rue de Nazareth." With the faith of Joseph and Mary knocking on doors trying to find a manger to stay in for the night—and a bit of luck—we rang the buzzer. Moments later, a man in his early 40s appeared, the owner of two apartments in the building—one for himself and his partner, the other for long-term holiday rentals. He led us through a quaint little courtyard and up a narrow, sturdy wooden staircase that spiraled upwards. Five flights later, through the tiny stairwell, we arrived at our destination.

There was a shared toilet in the hallway—quaint in that way only Parisian apartments can get away with—and a tiny pied-à-terre to the right. As he fumbled with the keys, we were buzzing with excitement. When the door creaked open, we walked into our summer palace. The space, though only 300 square feet, was vibrant with bright greens and yellows, and there was a tiny kitchenette tucked into one corner. A lofted bed overlooked the entire room—our little castle in the sky. It was perfect.

After signing the lease and stumbling through what little French we knew, we received the keys to our freedom. Jess and I couldn't contain our excitement—we ran around the apartment, screaming in joy, flung open the windows, and let the sunlight flood our new world. This was it. We had made it.

I quickly unpacked, tore photos from *Vogue,* and plastered the walls with images that inspired me. We took to the streets, found the local grocery store, Monoprix, and stocked up on essentials: Coca-Cola, baguettes, and pudding (which, as it turns out, would be my diet for the entire summer). Between us, I had a couple hundred euros, but Jess had even less—so a budget was key. We'd need to ration every cent if we wanted to last until the end of summer.

But it almost didn't matter. We were living in France. Two bohemians living in an attic, with a world full of adventure out our front door. Every time we stepped onto the Parisian streets, we were overwhelmed by the magic of it all. The city felt like an extension of my soul, and I couldn't stop thinking, *"Oh my God, we're really here."*

The next day, I found my French language school, just two blocks away in Place de la République, and started attending classes daily. But learning French with dyslexia? Let's just say it was a special kind of torture. I thought it'd be more conversational, something I could pick up on the go, but the endless conjugations and formal rules tripped me up at every turn. Determined to make it work, I picked up the *Harry Potter* books in French at a local bookstore. Since I knew every line by heart in English, I could practically guess what the French version was saying, which made it feel a little more familiar. It was like a cheat code, slowly helping me push past the usual dyslexia hurdles—but it was still a battle I had to face every single day.

Turns out, the school also offered digital arts, photography, and painting classes in the afternoon. That had all been part of my college workload, so I thought, *"C'est la vie!"* When in Paris, might as well pick up a camera and a paintbrush, right? Jess, who was studying art at her university, joined in, and we'd spend afternoons exploring Paris with sketchbooks and cameras in hand, getting lost in the beauty around us. I was determined to capture the city through my lens—every little corner and cobblestone street. Digital cameras had just come into vogue, and with my trusty little Canon 64-something, I was snapping shots of everything, each photo feeling like I'd struck gold.

The summer was shaping up to be magical, but that magic came with a price. Class fees and groceries were slowly cutting into our funds. I'd paid in advance for our apartment, but the day-to-day costs were climbing. I knew if we wanted to make it till the fall, we'd need extra spending cash. "How long can a baguette last?" I looked over at Jess with a questioning face. We quickly cut out the puddings.

Jess, meanwhile, was already taking action. She'd been visiting every English pub within walking distance, asking if they needed help during the days while I was in class. But our options were slim—French wasn't our strong suit, and most places turned us away before we even had a chance to explain. Every "Non, merci" made our situation feel a little more precarious. We were in Paris, yes, but the dream was getting expensive fast.

As we darted carefreely around the corners of the 10th arrondissement, life back in Iowa was changing in ways we hadn't anticipated. Our sister Heidi and Jill were flying over to join us, but not for reasons anyone would have wished. Jill had fled France some years earlier, escaping what had become a fractured fairy tale—an abusive marriage in a quaint provincial town in southern France. The cobblestone streets and charming cafés that had once felt like the setting of a dream now stood in stark contrast to the harsh reality she had endured.

In a scene that felt straight out of *Not Without My Daughter,* Jill packed up her life while her husband was at work, dropping plastic bags of clothes out of the window of their three-story apartment building. If anyone questioned her, it needed to look like she was just going to the laundromat. She left the rest of her life behind. With a two-year-old and four-year-old in tow, she hailed a cab to a nearby abbey. This wasn't some grand cathedral—no, it was a quiet, safe haven, hidden away like a secret. With its worn stone walls and carved 18th-century arches, the abbey provided her with sanctuary, a place to regroup as she plotted her escape.

She wanted to flee to the States, but her husband had hidden the kids' passports, leaving her trapped with no way forward and no way back. There she was, in the middle of this picturesque French town, feeling like the star of her own novel—only this time, the stakes were all too real. A friend snuck over to the abbey in the dead of night, handed her a bag with $5,000 in cash—her only lifeline—hugged her tightly, and slipped away. Jill spent the rest of the night wide awake, unable to sleep, gripped by the fear of missing their early morning flight.

When they arrived at the airport, plastic bags in hand, she knew they needed to look "normal." So she darted into the nearest gift shop, grabbed the first piece of luggage she saw, and stuffed the bags inside. Her mom, Mrs. Connors—the neighbor with the greenhouse—had contacted a consulate officer, who agreed to help. He asked Mrs. Connors, "Can she act?" "She was president of her high school Thespian troupe," her mom replied. "She'll figure it out!"

Jill rolled up to the ticket counter and explained to the woman that their passports had gone missing that morning while they were staying at the "hotel." She acted distraught with her best dramatic flair. The ticket agent, who barely spoke a word of English, called the consulate officer. Jill watched as the agent struggled with the conversation, exasperated by the technical jargon the consulate officer was throwing at her. Finally, the agent handed her the phone—a stroke of luck. Jill took over, answering a series of "verification" questions—birthdays, Social Security numbers—while the agent nodded along. Without another word, the agent, clearly relieved, handed over three boarding passes. The hardest part was over.

But then Jill's heart stopped. At the gate, armed soldiers patrolled with automatic rifles. She was convinced her husband had found her. Skirting by, hiding her face, her nerves were shot.

She didn't fully relax until the plane took off. Somewhere over the Atlantic, she took her first real breath, kissed her kids, ordered a drink, and tilted it heavenward. When they landed in the United States, Jill's mom, family, and our neighbors were anxiously waiting. They brought clothes, toys, and everything Jill needed to start over. Because starting over was exactly what they were doing.

However, the nightmare rarely ends there. Six months later, at her grandmother's funeral, sitting quietly with her children in a carved wooden church pew, Jill glanced back only to find her husband sitting behind her, uninvited. Calmly, he whispered, "I know where you live." It was like Sleeping with the Enemy all over again. She knew she had to finalize the divorce, but to do that, she had to go back to France.

Since I was already living in Paris, we arranged for her to use my address for mail and legal documents while she sorted things out. Jess and I helped her find an apartment down the street, playing the role of Parisian experts, living the dream in our little pied-à-terre. Heidi wanted to help Jill and her kids, so she flew over to help them settle in for their summer away from home. On paper, everything seemed perfect.

As Jill and the kids set up their new life, Heidi stayed with us in our studio for two weeks. It worked out well since she had saved up for a holiday and didn't need a hotel, so she pitched in with our day-to-day expenses. Thank God, because now we could at least afford puddings again. Determined to take on Paris in style, Heidi would set out with us in the mornings before I went to class, her short black hair in a bob, bundled up under a French beret she'd bought at a corner shop. It was her first time out of the country, so the trip doubled as a vacation for her. Back home, she had been freelance writing, and when she decided to come with Jill, she pitched her editor an assignment to write an article on French wineries. Naturally, she reached out to one of the best—Moët & Chandon— and was invited for a tour! The three of us, the ragtag crew from Dubuque, Iowa, made plans for a day trip to the vineyards of Moët, having no idea what we were in for.

We imagined a quaint vineyard tour, maybe a glass or two of wine before catching the train back. I didn't even really know what Moët was, but I knew I already loved it. After a short train ride out of Paris, the rolling hills of the French countryside unfolded before us, and we arrived at what looked like a literal palace. A butler in white gloves opened the door of our Peugeot, greeted us with a formal bow, and said, "Welcome to the Chateau de Napoleon." He explained this was where Napoleon himself once lived, and I remember thinking,

"Wait, what?"

We were instantly aware we'd underestimated this "quaint tour." The butler politely asked, "Would you like to change?" Jess, Heidi, and I exchanged wide-eyed glances, confused. "Change?" We looked down at our jeans and tennis shoes, thinking this would be a casual day trip. But no, it wasn't a tour—they had arranged a twelve-course meal for honored guests. A meal fit for royalty, or at least the French aristocracy who somehow survived the Revolution.

Here we were—three American kids rolling up to Napoleon's chateau, thinking we'd sip a little wine and be on our way. Instead, we were escorted into a grand parlor where France's elite mingled: the country's top jockey, a group of wine connoisseurs from Austria, and people who looked like they belonged in the pages of *Town & Country* magazine. And then there was us, decked out in jean jackets and t-shirts. The clash of worlds couldn't have been more stark.

We were soon ushered into a lavish dining room with a table that seemed to stretch for miles. Gilded china, crystal champagne flutes sparkling under chandeliers—it was wealth beyond anything I'd ever seen. I was snapping pictures with my little Canon digital camera, trying to take it all in. The first course arrived, and with it, champagne. It wasn't just a glass, though—there was a different champagne for every course. "Heidi, this is crazy!" I whispered. "Do you even know what foie gras is?" It was like something straight out of a Disney movie: *"Try the gray stuff. It's delicious."* Jess, champagne in hand, giggled and chimed in: *"Don't believe me? Ask the dishes!"*

Before long, there were five different glasses of champagne lined up in front of us, each for a different course. By the second course, I was already tipsy, laughing with Jess and snapping more pictures. The French elite barely acknowledged our presence; after all, we couldn't even speak to them, and I'm sure we stuck out like sore thumbs. Jess, also feeling the effects of the champagne, leaned over to me, "OMG. How are WE even here!? This meal easily costs more than either of us has in our bank accounts!" I mean, the Tonys were one thing—we felt like we belonged there. But this? This was a completely different level of luxury—*old-world* money—and maybe for the first time, we realized just how hilariously out of our league (and dreams) we were.

We were drowning in a champagne fountain of riches, but for everyone else, it was like drinking water—just another day for the bourgeois at Napoleon's chateau.

The event organizer leaned over to Heidi, asking in perfect English, "Who do you write for?" Probably privately hoping she worked for *Food & Wine* magazine, *The New York Times* or at very least *The DesMoines Register*. And Heidi, in true Midwestern form, replied, "Oh, me? I work for *The Field Guide* blog." At that moment, I nearly choked on my champagne. A blog! We were sitting in Napoleon's dining hall with the French aristocracy, and our credentials boiled down to a humble Iowa blog—a playful nod to cornfields and small-town charm. I could barely contain myself.

After endless courses and champagne, we retired to another parlor for cognac, but I was ready to wave my white flag—I couldn't drink another drop. Practically tripping over ourselves, Jess, Heidi, and I were finally escorted out of the chateau and back into the Peugeot, en route to the train station. In the rearview mirror, I could see the butler, nose tilted to the sun, dusting the dirt off his perfectly white gloves. As the car pulled away, I could almost hear his parting thought, dismissing us with the same aristocratic flair as Marie Antoinette: *"Let them eat cake."* And for the first time in our lives, we certainly had. We laughed all the way back, rolling through the French countryside on the train, still giddy from the absurdity of it all.

The entire experience was surreal—a strange juxtaposition of the life we'd come from, once scheming to win a Cap'n Crunch sweepstakes, to suddenly sitting in the castle of one of the world's greatest emperors, Napoleon. It felt like a moment where past and future starkly collided—a couple of underdog kids from Iowa chasing a cartoon captain had led them into a world they'd never imagined. Watching these nobles marvel at the masterpieces on the walls, the frescoes, the gilded molding, eager to own it all, my mind spun, thinking about what art and photography could mean to me. That afternoon was more than a meal—it was the opening of a doorway into a kind of riches I hadn't even dared to dream of, and with that, the faintest embers of a new path flickered in the back of my mind.

But the magic of that moment didn't last. No sooner had Heidi flown back to Iowa than reality came crashing back in. Jess and I had finished school, and we were walking back to the apartment when I noticed a man sitting in the dark corner of the hallway. Something about him sent a chill down my spine. He was just sitting there, in the shadows. I greeted him, American-style, with a "Hey!" and immediately realized my mistake—I should've said "Bonjour."

He looked up at me and said in a low voice, "I know who you are."

It hit me like a brick—this was Jill's husband.

I grabbed Jess by the arm, and we bolted up the stairs, my heart racing. As we fumbled to unlock the apartment door, I dialed Jill, my voice completely panicked, rushing to warn her. "Jill! Don't come over, he's here!" We bolted the door and locked ourselves inside, hoping the walls would keep the nightmare at bay. But only seconds later, the loud banging started.

"Open up! It's the police!"

Jess and I were panicking, trapped in our 300-square-foot studio with the police banging on the door as if we were harboring a fugitive. We let them in, and I desperately tried to explain—using my broken mix of French and English—that Jess wasn't Jill, that she was my sister. "Welcome to my chateau! Would you like a drink?" I stammered, trying to diffuse the situation, but the police were in no mood for pleasantries.

They began searching the place, flipping through our meager belongings as if they expected to find hidden children in our cramped loft. The lofted bedroom upstairs overlooked the small living space, and I couldn't believe they were tearing through it like it was some secret lair. I kept repeating, "She's not Jill, I swear!" but they didn't seem to believe me. Eventually, they relented, realizing Jess wasn't the woman they were after—but not before rattling us both to the core.

Later that night, Jill called. Her voice trembled on the other end of the line. "Luke, I don't know what to do. If he's back... I can't stay here with the kids. We can't sit here waiting for him to find us. He's bound to find out I'm just down the street."

"I know. I talked to my mom, she's at your parents' house, and we'll figure something out," I said, glancing at Jess, who was eavesdropping, her face tight with worry. "We'll help you get out."

"I just... I thought I was safe here." Her voice cracked. The desperation was palpable.

"You are. He still doesn't know where you live—just where I live. That's the best thing we've got going for us right now," I reassured her. "You just need to lay low for a few days... maybe let's go out of town?"

There was a pause, and then Jess piped up, "Disneyland. She could take them to Disneyland Paris! He'd never look there, right?"

"That's it," Jill said, a note of hope creeping in. "We can disappear there for the weekend, at least."

"OK," I agreed. "We'll get you out early tomorrow. I'll meet you outside at 6 AM. Jess can keep an eye on the street to make sure it's clear. I'll meet you in front of your building, grab the kids' luggage, and get you all into a cab. If Jess sees an officer, she'll call to warn you not to leave the apartment."

Jill took a deep breath. "Thank you. Really. For everything."

The next morning, we snuck her and the kids out with only what they could carry. Their escape wasn't some high-speed car chase, but the tension in the air made it feel just as dramatic. The kids were bundled into a cab, and off they went to catch a train, with Jill whispering promises to her children that everything would be fine. They disappeared into the Parisian morning fog, leaving me standing there, adrenaline coursing through my veins. It felt like we had dodged a bullet.

Disneyland Paris became her refuge, the place she could vanish for a few days, lost among the crowds of tourists. It was a strange and almost surreal plan, hiding from an abusive ex-husband in the happiest place on Earth, but it was the best option we had.

For the next few days, Jill and her kids wandered through Disneyland, mingling with tourists, riding roller coasters, and pretending everything was normal. It was a bizarre juxtaposition, hiding from a dangerous man while meeting Mickey Mouse and enjoying the spinning teacups. Meanwhile, Jess and I kept low in the Marais, hoping we wouldn't see her husband lurking in the shadows of Rue de Nazareth again.

Eventually, after a week spent at Disneyland Paris, Jill returned. Her husband, for now, was out of the picture, but the fear he had instilled in her lingered like a ghost. Over the next six months, she fought tooth and nail through the French legal system, securing her divorce and finally breaking free of him for good.

Jess had never been able to find work, and my savings were no longer enough to support us both. Through all of our ups and downs, we had been trying everything to make our finances work. We pounded the cobblestones of Paris, café after café, and even the local tourist shops. Walking into each place with that wide-eyed Iowa charm, trying her best French to ask if they needed extra help. But everywhere we went, it was the same: "Non, merci."

I was quickly looking at my credit card limit as a backup (cha-ching). We had survived this long on very little money—what was a tiny bit of debt? However, cutting out *café crèmes* for a midday treat at the sidewalk bistros was next on the list of things we'd have to do without. By August, the carefree days of exploring Paris felt like a distant memory, and the looming fear of running out of money weighed on us constantly. The idea of stretching another month in the city was slipping away fast.

When Jess left early, it felt like all the life and laughter drained from our little attic apartment. The streets of the Marais, once so full of wonder, felt quieter without her by my side. My Parisian fairytale began to unravel, and the city that once seemed like a dream was starting to shift quickly into reality. I'd sit by the small window, watching the world go by, trying to piece together a plan, as chatter I still struggled to understand floated up from the street below.

Alone in that tiny apartment, haunted by rejection and the emptiness left by Jess's departure—and still processing the ordeal with Jill's husband—a creeping loneliness settled in. I had to rethink my plan of possibly staying in Paris longer.

Sitting in that silent room, staring out at the gray Parisian streets that once seemed so full of promise, I came to a conclusion. The next day, I booked a plane ticket back to New York City, packed up my life in Paris, and rented out the apartment to a classmate. By the first week of September, I was home, back in the city, a bit of a stranger in a strange land.

But I arrived in New York with my suitcases filled not with clothes and keepsakes from France, but with something much more unexpected—a creative obsession. I had become captivated by the city itself, taking endless photos of the Eiffel Tower's iron lattice and the streets, marveling at how they seemed to change with the light, the weather, and even my mood. And though I was leaving Paris, I wasn't ready to let go of that glow just yet.

As I unpacked and went through all my photos, I felt inspired. Remembering what I'd learned from Jess during our classes that summer, I picked up a paintbrush, thinking, *If she could be so good, maybe I had a bit of that magic in me too.* I bought some canvases and started painting Paris—the Eiffel Tower, the bridges over the Seine at dusk, the city in all its moods, shapes, and colors. Using a mix of paintbrushes, digital photos, my graphic design background, and an old 1950s overhead projector I'd snagged on eBay—the kind with a magnifying arm and lightbulb—I brought a pop art vision of Paris to life. If I couldn't live in the City of Lights, I would bring the lights home.

Laura, my friend who had been there for me through so much, was now running a grant program called the Starving Artists Ball. She was juggling everything for the show—coordinating dozens of artists, setting up photographers, arranging entertainment, and organizing all the fundraising logistics. When she saw my work, she told me I had to submit it. I thought she was just being nice, but no—Laura was serious. She was so impressed with what I'd done in my short time back that she put my work up in front of the committee to be considered for the show. And, to my utter surprise, I got approved.

That was my first art show. There I was, running away from one dream and accidentally stumbling into another. The Starving Artists Ball was no ordinary exhibition—it was *the* event, a decadent fundraising gala that drew in all kinds of creative souls and art collectors. Held in a sprawling, candlelit Lower East Side synagogue where Sarah Jessica Parker got married. The space shimmered in a deep red light, casting a kind of magical glow over everything. The vaulted ceilings echoed with soft whispers and clinking glasses, while the scent of wine and possibility filled the air. Outwardly, I looked like a beacon of confidence, but inside, I was a nervous wreck—still that little boy wondering when the bullies were going to pounce. I had been painting for less than a few months; surely someone would see I was a fraud?

Yet my paintings—humble attempts to hold onto the fleeting magic of Paris—were now the talk of the evening. Seeing them there, surrounded by the warm glow of candles and the buzz of people who actually wanted to talk about them, made me feel like I'd stepped into a storybook of my own. Each face that wandered over brought a jolt of excitement, and when they asked about the pieces, I launched into my Paris tales like a tour guide, describing every moment I'd tried to capture on canvas.

And then came the first sale. My jaw nearly hit the floor when someone just had to have one. Then another person came up, and another—until I'd sold every single piece! It wasn't riches, but it was three times the amount of money I'd left for Paris with, and to me, that was a million-dollar feeling.

That night, as I looked around at the bustling party and the faces of people who'd invested in my art for the first time, I felt like I'd stumbled onto something extraordinary. Walking out of that glowing room, a couple of paintings lighter, I realized: *Maybe don't be afraid to follow a dream—it might just take you places you never planned on going.*

It made me think that real success is measured by the people we choose to stand beside when everything else is crumbling. I had done that for Jill, and Laura was doing that for me now. Sometimes, dreams don't just slip away—they fall apart in the most unexpected ways. And yet, when I jumped, it wasn't just me standing there—I had friends to help me find my footing again.

Life had a funny way of pulling me back up just when I thought I'd tripped and fallen all over those cobblestone streets on Rue de Nazareth. But I had learned a few things along the way: don't be afraid to take risks, trust in the people who believe in you, and, yes, always keep a good outfit in your bag—you never know when you'll end up at a château.

Chapter 6
The Volcano Goddess

This is just an interlude, a respite before the storm—a myth, a far-flung fantasy, a story of princes and gods and wicked stepchildren, the kind with cursed tiki idols and lore that may or may not have really happened. So, with that in mind...

Once upon a time, deep in the shimmering glass canyons of New York City, there was a boy who found himself swallowed by the monotonous grind of an office job—a modern-day handmaiden of sorts, a secretary to the bourgeoisie. His task wasn't chimney sweeping but the monotonous drone of filing papers and answering phones, day in and day out. Every keystroke felt like a slow fade from the dreams of Parisian streets he once knew. Maybe he'd never get rich, but he could live, even if scraping by, as long as there was adventure at hand...

My life had had its glamorous twists and turns, and from the outside, it might have even looked fancy, but packaging is a cheap façade, and that ever-elusive money scheme I'd chased as a kid was slipping further from my grasp.

My boss was no French nobleman. He was a wealthy (slightly arrogant) man who ran the company alongside his husband, a figure with a hairstyle so white, so meticulously coiffed into a pompadour, you'd swear it had been powdered, giving him the air of an aristocrat who'd just stepped out of a château. Together, they moved through life as if they were Manhattan royalty, carrying a sense of privilege as if it were their birthright. His family was one of those whose names rang with legacy—like the Rockefellers or the Kennedys—and their world was all lavish dinner parties, European vacations, and exclusive galas.

Maybe I was dripping with envy and jealousy, but as I watched them live in this bubble of wealth and status, I began to realize I wanted something more than just money. Paris had sparked something within me—a hunger for purpose, for creativity, for a life that wasn't always real. I felt stifled, under the wicked gaze of two ugly stepsisters, chained to a desk while dreaming of a world beyond the gray tower windows of Manhattan, a world where I could finally be free to chase yet another dream.

One afternoon, as fate would have it, like a mischievous little woodland creature, curiosity got the better of me. The office was quiet as a mouse; everyone had left for the day, and I found myself clicking around on my villainous little boss's computer. I wasn't looking for anything in particular, just spying to speed along the ticking of the clock. But what I stumbled upon shook me straight out of my proverbial glass slippers—his search history.

There it was, clear as the morning sun: a linked file from a site called Badpuppy. I hesitated for a moment, my finger hovering over the mouse, thinking I might be caught on a secret camera. But then, like every bad decision ever made, curiosity won out. I clicked.

And that's when the punch landed. Boom, boom, boom— there, on the screen, was Striker Christiansen. My heart started racing. Striker Christiansen wasn't just some random sexy, shirtless Hollywood prince; it was... Christian. My Christian. My first love, the boy I had spent hidden summer nights with, the one I thought about far more often than I should have. Except now, Christian had become a star—a steamy adult film star, but still! A boy so famous that my snooty little boss had saved my ex-boyfriend's videos to his desktop!

I could've died. The memories of our secret rendezvous, the summer heat, the way we'd sneak away to steal a kiss under the stars—all flooded back while watching the movie. A pool boy, cutting grass, whisked away by some handsome Latin duke! But now, Christian—er, Striker—was someone larger than life, someone playing a part I, on occasion, still dreamt about. He was no longer the boy I'd kissed in cornfields. He had become gay royalty. I stared at the screen, frozen, while my mind wrestled with this new version of him. It would've been erotic if I wasn't sitting in the middle of my boss's office! (Okay, it was still erotic.)

Unable to process what I was feeling, I did what any scandal-prone, gossip-loving twenty-something would do: I reached out to an old friend from high school. And with that one phone call, I unknowingly unleashed a whirlwind of gossip, drama, and chaos into the kingdom that would spiral into yet another fairytale of my life. As we used to say during those backstage nights performing *Grease*, I had really kicked up some "Drama-lama ding dong"—and the fireworks were about to explode all over again. Boom. Boom. Boom.

But just as I was beginning to unravel from a new mess, a lifeline appeared. Laura and her best friend Mayumi threw down a long golden rope from the tower and extended an invitation I couldn't refuse—a trip to their homeland of Hawai'i, a land of mythical gods and giants. Mayumi, as stunning and fair as a maiko, with sleek black hair cut at a sharp angle that framed her face, was heading home to visit family, and Laura had a wedding to attend. I wasn't about to pass up a chance to see the breathtaking islands. Only catch? I'd be the designated photographer for the bridal party. Easy! Hands down, yes. Escaping the office grind and the storm I'd kicked up? Agreeing was as easy as climbing a beanstalk. Sign me up. I was eager to meet Laura's family and dive headfirst into an adventure that promised to be unforgettable. It was time, once again, to set off for another wonderland.

The promise of Hawai'i felt like exactly what I needed. Mayumi and I flew out early to Oahu—her boyfriend worked for Delta and scored us buddy passes, so my ticket was basically free, costing me only a few magic beans for taxes and luggage. Plus, we were both crashing on the floor of the wedding hotel, making this trip cost next to nothing—just the low, low price of capturing the island's beauty through my lens, which was about what I had in my savings account. Count me in!

— PELE AND HER FORBIDDEN PARADISE —

Our days on Oahu were filled with one adventure after another. I marveled at the tide pools, feeling like I had become a marine biologist, captivated by the colorful life hiding in the shallows. One day, while exploring the shoreline near the rocks, Mayumi pointed out these delicate half-bloomed flowers. She called them *Naupaka*.

Curious, I asked, "Why does it only have half its petals?"

Mayumi smiled and shared the legend she had been told: "Naupaka was a beautiful princess who fell deeply in love with Kaui, a humble fisherman. Their love was forbidden, and when the couple sought the advice of a kahuna, or priest, they were told they could never be together. Some say it was because their love defied the sacred laws of tradition; others whisper it was because Naupaka was Pele's sister, and the goddess of fire had grown jealous of their affection.

Enraged by their defiance, Pele pursued Kaui up the mountain and deep into the forest, her fiery wrath scorching the earth beneath her feet. As the flames closed in around him, the gods intervened, transforming Kaui into the Naupaka kuahiwi—a mountain flower with only half its petals. Furious and frustrated, Pele turned her attention to Naupaka, who had sought refuge among the rocks by the shore. Before she could strike, the gods rescued the princess, transforming her into the Naupaka kahakai, a seaside flower that also bore only half a bloom.

Separated by fire and distance, the two lovers were forever torn apart, their bond marked by the two halves of the Naupaka flower. Mayumi went on to explain that the Naupaka flowers themselves always appear incomplete—split in half. One grows in the mountains and the other by the sea, but when brought together, they fit perfectly, symbolizing the love that Naupaka and Kaui could never fully realize."

And that was the moment I felt it—that was when I fell in love with this island.

But I wasn't done falling head over heels yet. The North Shore—famous for its big waves and laid-back surfer vibe—was a place I'd always dreamed of visiting, and it's where we decided to take our first surfing lesson.

Our instructor, a sun-kissed local boy with an easy charm, had me goo-goo-eyed from the moment he flashed that smile. Honestly, I couldn't hear a word he said; I was too busy watching his every move. He tossed our soft-top boards into the back of his truck, and we sped down the winding roads of the North Shore, my heart racing with anticipation. On the beach, he walked us through the basics—how to pop up, keep our balance—and while I felt confident on land, the water was a different story.

Paddling was brutal. The board was too wide, and my arms turned to jelly within minutes. Every stroke felt impossible, but

Mayumi and I were determined. Our instructor cheered us on from his board with a casual, "Good job, dude!" His encouragement (and muscles) made my heart skip a beat, and I pushed through the exhaustion, desperate to impress him. Suddenly, a massive sea turtle glided beneath us near Turtle Bay, and for a moment, the struggle didn't matter. It felt like pure magic.

Mayumi stood up on her first wave like a pro, thanks to the instructor's steady guidance. I, however, had to psych myself up: "Man up—impress this guy!" After a few spectacular wipeouts, I finally found my balance and stood up. For a brief, glorious moment, I felt like a real surfer. The instructor let out a loud whoop, and my cheeks flushed bright red. Right then and there, I could've surfed forever.

— ONE —

Later, left to my own devices, I met him. He looked like the quintessential beach bum: tropical tan, carefree dirty blond hair falling over his face, and hazel eyes half-hidden beneath the salty, sun-kissed mess. Even his nose ring gave him an edge, like some mythical minotaur brought to life. We exchanged glances along the shore, and before long, we were sharing Mai Tais at a tiki bar in Waikiki. Everything felt easy, natural—the kind of connection that only seems possible in a place as magical as this. Between sips and the lulling sound of waves outside, our conversation flowed effortlessly, each story pulling us closer.

As the night wore on and the drinks piled up, our laughter grew louder, the chemistry undeniable. At one point, he leaned in, a mischievous grin lighting up his face.

"You know what would make this night even better?" he asked, fishing through his bag.

"What?" I asked, half-laughing, expecting some cheesy line.

He held up a small pill, whispering dramatically, "Muscle relaxers."

"Muscle relaxers?" I repeated, raising an eyebrow.

"Trust me, they're amazing," he said, shaking the pill like a magic trick. "You'll feel like you're floating on this island."

"In that case," I said, clinking my glass against his with a laugh. "Why not?"

It seemed like a good idea at the time—or maybe that was the Mai Tais talking. One thing led to another, and I found myself crashing in his tiny bedroom at the gay hostel. You'd think it was a dream, but I was in no condition to walk, talk, or... well, muscle relaxers aren't exactly uppers.

The next morning hit like an alarm I didn't set. I woke tangled in his sheets, grabbed my clothes, kissed his groggy face one last time, and stumbled out into the harsh light of reality, nursing a headache that could rival a hurricane.

By the time we reached the Big Island, reconnecting with Laura to continue the wedding adventure, I was back on my feet. Laura was eager to show me the island's famous volcano, and the thought of standing before nature's fiery power filled me with a mix of excitement and dread. As we drove through rolling fields of hardened lava—black and glittering under the sun like a lunar landscape—it felt like we were on the edge of another world.

After a three-hour drive, we finally reached the volcano, and I... I was underwhelmed. "What? It's just a giant hole in the ground!" I thought. The flat expanse of black rock and lazy smoke drifting from the crater didn't match my blockbuster expectations. The acrid smell of sulfur stung the back of my throat, unsettling but not dramatic. I wanted lava, explosions, something worthy of a movie scene.

"How can we make this more exciting?" I asked Laura, half-joking. "Pretend you're Pele, goddess of fire and volcanoes! Dance around the offerings so I can get some epic shots."

Scattered across the blackened ground were offerings to Pele—fruits, flowers, even bottles of beer—left by locals hoping to appease the ancient goddess. Laura rolled her eyes but humored me, posing dramatically in front of the offerings. Mayumi, however, looked uneasy.

"You don't want to mess with Pele," she said, half-serious. "You guys are in for it now."

As we left, the air was thick with laughter and jokes about Pele's revenge. I shrugged it off, too caught up in the incredible shots I'd captured to realize what I had done—or the trouble I'd just invited.

— TWO —

We pulled up to the wedding and were greeted by the sight of a lavish resort that felt like it had been carved straight out of the volcanic rock. The Mauna Kea beach hotel was an old-style Hawaiian monolith, towering majestically over the coastline, drenched in history and luxury. Gold Buddhas stood regally in the corners, their serene expressions reflecting the tranquility of the island, while beautiful vintage Hawaiian quilts hung proudly from the walls, adding a warm, authentic touch. The air smelled of plumeria and sea salt, and everything about the place whispered opulence and serenity.

I couldn't help but marvel at the setting's elegance. Everything should have been perfect. But as the welcome dinner unfolded, an unsettling feeling began to creep in—an itch that I couldn't quite place. At first, I brushed it off, thinking maybe it was the humidity or nerves before the big event. I kept scratching absentmindedly throughout the night, but as the evening went on, it became harder to ignore. By dessert, the itch had turned into a full-blown distraction, and people were starting to notice.

What was happening? I racked my brain, trying to figure out what could possibly be causing this relentless irritation. A reaction to the tropical flowers? An allergic response to the linens? The hot tub? I tossed and turned that night, the lavish Hawaiian quilts no longer offering the comfort they promised.

By the next morning, it hit me—like a horrifying revelation from a bad detective novel. Crabs. Crabs! I looked down and I had crabs! My skin crawled, both literally and figuratively. The mystery was solved, and I traced it back with grim certainty: muscle-relaxer boy, my handsome little minotaur, and his sketchy hostel. Of course. Fantastic.

So, there I was at this fancy resort, scratching like crazy, trying to act normal during the pre-wedding brunch while internally freaking out. Desperate, I grabbed some overpriced shaving cream from the hotel gift shop (cha-ching) and swiped an mandarin orange towel from the pool attendant while his back was turned. I slinked into the spa locker room, darted to the farthest stall, huddled in the corner, and proceeded to shave every stray hair from my entire body in an attempt to rid myself of the little critters. Legs, armpits, everything. With hair circling the drain, I must've looked ridiculous—like some kind of half-crazed, soaking wet, wrinkly-skinned hairless cat. Trust me, it was one of the worst experiences of my life.

With my clean-shaven, itchy body hidden beneath the Aloha shirt I'd picked up at Ross Dress for Less, the cheap fabric scratched against my now razor-irritated skin. Somehow, I made it through the ceremony. The wedding was beautiful, and the champagne flowed freely—which, in hindsight, was a bad idea for someone already so frazzled. At least I'd stopped scratching, so none of the guests were any the wiser.

As the reception hit full swing, the tequila shots started flowing. Determined to keep the energy high, I made it my mission to order rounds for everyone. Before long, the entire wedding party was wasted, dancing wildly under the stars. The photos I captured were pure magic—the dance floor lights swirling in vibrant colors, blurring into the haze of the night. You could almost feel the tequila-soaked revelry seeping through the film, with each shot reflecting the joyful chaos of the evening. Once the dancing wrapped up, someone had the brilliant idea to hit the beach, and before I knew it, Laura, in all her effervescent splendor, was stripping down and sprinting toward the ocean. "Back in the day, my grandma used to call this flanging!" she shouted, launching herself into the air, arms spread wide, and crashing naked into the waves. Naturally, the rest of the wedding party followed suit, racing into the surf with all the grace of a herd of stumbling wildebeests, shedding clothes and inhibitions along the way.

The tide was playing tricks that night. It rolled in with deceptive gentleness, luring everyone into a false sense of confidence. One after another, naked butts sprinted toward the water, only for the waves to pull back at the last second, leaving them jumping headlong into wet sand. It was like a slapstick comedy, watching them leap with abandon, only to crash face-first as the ocean retreated. The moonlight shimmered off the flat expanse, amplifying the absurdity of people crawling to the surf, as each new runner repeated the same mistake, over and over.

Caught up in the laughter and chaos, I couldn't resist joining in. I ran full tilt into the disaster, completely forgetting the small but crucial detail that I had shaved my entire body earlier that day. The moment I hit the water, I realized how out of place I was—there I stood, hairless and gleaming under the moonlight, like a glowing pale naked mole rat stranded in a sea of normal, saltwater-soaked bodies. The waves continued their teasing retreat, and I was left exposed, a shining, hairless oddity in the vast expanse of the ocean.

Of course, as if the night couldn't get any crazier, the police showed up. Flashlights waving, they chased us out of the water, but thankfully, they brought beach towels for everyone. Feeling particularly self-conscious about getting caught in the patrolmen's piercing searchlights, especially in my hairless state, I shouted at Laura to grab me a towel. She motioned me over, and when I thought salvation was in sight, I realized—she didn't have a towel for me! Panicked and mortified, I scrambled to hide behind a row of beach chairs, crouching low as if I could somehow disappear into the sand. My heart raced, and every second felt like an eternity. Just when I thought I might have to sprint back to the hotel naked, a hotel attendant pitched a bright orange pool towel straight at me, smacking me right in the face. I quickly wrapped it around myself, grateful to finally be covered but still feeling the burn of humiliation.

The night hit its low point as I passed out on the beach, slumped in a lawn chair, vomiting from a cocktail of tequila and salt water. The waves churned in the distance, but the real storm was brewing inside me. Eventually, I dragged my sorry self to Laura's room, where I collapsed on the floor and passed out cold.

— THREE —

The alarm blared at 8 a.m., dragging me from the depths of tequila-induced hell. Barely functioning, I stumbled to the airport for an early flight back to Honolulu. How I even made it there remains one of life's great mysteries. On the plane, I was seated next to a cheerful woman from Iowa—of all places—and struck up a conversation to distract myself from the nausea still swirling in my stomach like a blender on high.

But halfway through the short 40-minute flight, disaster struck. Mid-sentence, I froze, eyes wide, and lunged for the air sickness bag. "Wreeeeech!" The sound was louder than the engines, echoing through the cabin as I filled the bag—and then another—while the poor woman looked on in abject horror. Mortified and drenched in sweat, I couldn't even bring myself to look at her.

As the plane descended into Honolulu, the sight of houses stacked on the mountainside—like concrete fingers clawing at the sky—felt oddly comforting. I had never been so relieved to see solid ground. Turning to my unfortunate seatmate, I mumbled a heartfelt apology and wobbled off the plane, convinced the worst was behind me.

It wasn't.

At the ticket counter, reality landed like a sucker punch. All flights to New York were full. No standby. No waiting list. Nothing. My heart sank as the airline employee shook her head with the dead-eyed indifference of someone who's ruined countless vacations before breakfast.

"But... there's gotta be something," I pleaded, desperation creeping into my voice. I tried reasoning, bargaining—begging—but it was no use. Without a seat, I was stranded. The realization hit like a tidal wave: no backup plan, no extra cash, no way out.

Standing there in the middle of the bustling terminal, it felt like the island itself was conspiring to keep me trapped. The hum of announcements, the clatter of luggage wheels, and the distant roar of departing planes all blurred into an oppressive cacophony.

"One extra day in paradise," I told myself, trying to stay calm. But deep down, I knew this wasn't paradise anymore. This was purgatory—a tropical trap I couldn't escape. Defeated, we cabbed it back into town and booked a hotel. (Swipe, cha-ching!)

— FOUR —

A day later and a dollar shorter, with a few hours to kill before a hopeful standby flight, I decided to take one last trip to the beach. The waves, the breeze, the sun—it all felt like a last-ditch attempt at closure, as if I could wrestle something meaningful from the chaos. I swam, snapped photos, and let the hours slip by in a haze of salty air and warm sand. For a moment, it almost felt like redemption.

But paradise, I should've known by now, doesn't let you leave without taking a piece of you with it.

I drifted off on the sand, lulled by the rhythm of the tide, only to wake in a panic. The water had rushed in, swallowing everything. My camera. My shoes. My bag. All of it. Scrambling, I clawed at the sand, grabbing what I could, but it was too late. My camera was soaked, its lens glistening with saltwater and totally lifeless. My phone? A bloated, waterlogged casualty. Drenched, defeated, and shoeless, I stumbled back to the hotel like a shipwreck survivor.

Mayumi took one look at me and shook her head, her voice dripping with unimpressed finality. "You've done it now, kid. Pele's got you. You best get home quick."

And honestly? At that point, I believed her. Between the volcano, the cursed trip, and this latest humiliation, it felt like every moment had been orchestrated by some vengeful goddess in dire need of a hobby.

But Pele wasn't done yet.

We returned to the airport, hoping for a miracle, but the standby list had swelled overnight like some cosmic joke. No flights to New York. Again. My patience was gone. My phone was still dead. And Pele's grip on my luck was unrelenting.

I opened my laptop, connected to the airport Wi-Fi, and scrolled through flights while angry emails from my boss pinged in the background. One-way. Direct. Outrageous. I hesitated for a moment—then clicked. (Cha-ching, cha-ching.) The most expensive flight of my life, but at that point, I didn't care. Pele had won.

— FIVE —

You'd think returning to the mainland would have made everything disappear, but no. For weeks, my boss seemed hell-bent on proving that misery could follow me anywhere. Every day felt like a battle—the little proletariat versus the big, bad aristocracy. He micromanaged my every move like a king inspecting peasants for crumbs.

Then came Valentine's Day: seventeen inches of snow buried the city, and I was stuck in bed with the flu, too sick to move, let alone fake productivity. That was it for him. He called me, seething, each word sharper than the icy wind rattling my windows. His condescending tone practically dripped through the receiver, soaking me in fresh humiliation.

I'd had it. No two weeks' notice, no farewell emails—I just quit. I pulled up Craigslist, sublet my room to the first taker, and started plotting my escape to a place where snow was just a distant memory: Honolulu. Surely, I thought, by now the gods had forgiven me—or at least forgotten me. I mean, after all, in my naivety, I had certainly forgotten them.

— SIX —

I traded the gray, slushy streets of Lower Manhattan for the sun-drenched shores of Waikiki, armed with a backpack, a dream, and exactly one surf lesson under my belt. My plan? Wait tables by night and surf by day, living out a postcard-perfect fantasy. My new roommate, Sven, a sun-kissed Swedish surfer I'd met online, picked me up in a rusted-out truck that looked like it had survived three hurricanes and a volcanic eruption. It had a surfboard rack strapped to the back, and he greeted me with a lei like we were in a rom-com. With his blond hair catching the light, I thought, *This is it. Paradise.*

The apartment, perched on the eighth floor of a quintessentially worn Honolulu building, *almost* lived up to the fantasy. The lobby had a faded dolphin mural straight out of the 1970s, and the wood-paneled elevator creaked and groaned its way to the eighth floor, making me wonder if we'd make it there alive. But the faint scent of plumeria wafted through the air, and that alone was enough to make me believe in magic. My "room" was the living room—a bare space with nothing but a blow-up mattress that deflated a little more with every move I made. But when I opened the glass sliding doors, the most breathtaking view of the city and the turquoise ocean sprawled out before me. Staring at the endless horizon, I leaned back on my bed, slowly sinking to the floor. It was perfect.

And then the rain came.

At first, it was charming—a light drizzle, the kind that makes you want to grab a ukulele and sing about rainbows. But by the next day, the sky decided it had *had enough* of that tropical postcard nonsense. Sheets of rain fell endlessly, as if the heavens had a grudge, transforming streets into rivers and beaches into muddy swamps. The lush greens of Hawai'i were drowning under the storm, sagging and defeated. For 40 straight days and nights, the rain didn't let up. The sky never cleared, and a thick gray haze settled over the islands like a bad mood.

Nothing was safe. Roads became whitewater rapids. Streams overflowed into neighborhoods. The ocean itself rose, crashing against the land with an attitude that said, "You thought this was paradise? Think again." Even inside the apartment, the damp was relentless—clothes refused to dry, mold made itself at home, and the air clung to your skin like a clammy handshake from someone you don't like. This wasn't just weather; this was a siege.

But Sven and I weren't about to let some biblical flood ruin our surfing dreams. Rain or shine—or hellfire and brimstone—we paddled out into the churning waves, determined to surf. The ocean, however, had other plans. Once warm and inviting, it had turned into a murky, angry soup of debris and bacteria. Runoff from the hills carried god-knows-what into the surf, and every wave felt like a slap in the face from Poseidon himself. Still, we paddled out, chasing a thrill as elusive as the sun.

It didn't take long for the consequences to catch up. I ignored the warning signs—a scratch here, a scrape there—until the universe decided to give me a full-on *lesson*. Bedridden with a staph infection, I found myself feverish, weak, and cursing my own stubbornness. Antibiotics became my new best friend, and yet, even as my body protested, I refused to let the rain win. Hawai'i wasn't paradise—it was a proving ground, a tropical boot camp designed by the gods to test how much punishment I could take.

And honestly? I wasn't sure who was winning.

— SEVEN —

One afternoon, healed but fed up with life's endless plot twists, I grabbed my board and decided to take on the storm, consequences be damned. The sky was a bruised shade of gray, thunder growling like it had a grudge, and the rain didn't just fall—it attacked, pelting me with stinging little bullets. The wind howled, whipping the palm trees into a frenzy. The ocean, meanwhile, looked like it was auditioning for a disaster movie, waves stacking up in a chaotic free-for-all.

But hey, why not? Soaked to the bone, freezing, and drenched in poor decision-making, I paddled out anyway. My arms burned, the wind screamed in my ears, and my board was tossed around like a chew toy for angry waves. Suddenly, something shot out of the air—sharp, fast—and hit me square in the chin. A fish? A piece of debris? I had no clue. All I knew was that it hurt like hell. My hand came away slick with blood, and the saltwater, ever the sadist, bit into the wound like it was adding insult to injury.

That was it. I'd had enough. The rain, the infections, the bad luck—it was like the gods were using me as their favorite voodoo doll. Glaring up at the stormy sky, I screamed, "I'm sorry, Pele! Just let me be!" The wind ripped my apology away, carrying it off to who-knows-where, as I paddled back to shore, utterly defeated.

By the time I dragged myself onto the sand, I realized my life had officially become a cursed Brady Bunch episode—the one where Greg steals the tiki idol and unleashes chaos. Only in my case, chaos came with stitches. Of course, the next logical stop was the hospital. Because, apparently, Hawai'i wasn't content to just break my spirit; it needed to break my chin, too.

— EIGHT —

Sven moved in with his girlfriend, leaving me to land a beachside sublet with roommates—a place that felt like paradise at first glance. The moment I moved in, I painted the walls a vibrant, sunset mango color that glowed at golden hour, transforming the space into the tropical island retreat of my dreams. My bed, draped in a rainbow-colored Pier One blanket, added the final touch to what I was certain was the perfect little sanctuary.

But paradise, as always, came with a catch: the night-time scratching and scurrying.

Living on the first floor in Hawai'i turned out to be a constant invitation for an army of bugs. Enormous, prehistoric-looking cockroaches and creeping centipedes emerged from the walls and floorboards the moment the sun went down, staking their claim on my so-called oasis.

Then came the fleas. Night after night, I woke up covered in bites. This wasn't the work of a stray mosquito—it was the feral cats that prowled the building's foundation like jungle royalty. Their fleas had made themselves at home, my dream sanctuary was becoming unlivable.

Determined to reclaim my space, I went full exterminator. Scrubbing floors with the fury of someone one flea bite away from losing it completely, I armed myself with a homemade concoction of Clorox and ammonia—because clearly, more chemicals meant more power. I attacked every corner of the apartment like I was on a mission to eradicate every bug in Hawai'i.

Instead of triumph, I unleashed toxic, eye-watering fumes that nearly took me out. My lungs burned like I'd inhaled fire, and before I knew it, I was stumbling outside, gasping for air on my way to the Minute Clinic. Turns out, I'd concocted a poison cocktail strong enough to fell an elephant. Lesson learned: next time, leave the chemical warfare to the professionals.

— NINE —

Fueled by frustration (and maybe a touch of delusion), I marched up to the landlord and demanded action. The bugs, the fleas—I wanted them gone. All of them. But my negotiating skills? Let's just say they had all the finesse of a bull in a china shop. The landlord not only refused to help but, in a move that hit with the subtlety of a freight train, managed to kick me out of the apartment entirely.

On my last morning there, I swung my feet over the side of the bed, ready to face one final day in my once-beloved sanctuary. And that's when I felt it. The floor was... alive. Maggots. Thousands of them. Crawling in waves like some hellish version of an ocean tide. I froze, horrified, as the nightmare unfolded beneath me, a grotesque scene straight out of a horror movie. At that moment, I knew: Pele, the Hawaiian goddess of fire and destruction, had hit me with her 11th-hour showstopper—ready to bring the house down.

This wasn't just a bad day—it was a full-on curse. The biblical plagues of Egypt had officially descended upon me. Muscle relaxers. Crabs. Canceled flights. A soaked camera. 40 days of rain. Infections. Stitches. Fleas. And now maggots. What could she possibly want next? My firstborn?! Honestly, at this point, I was convinced I'd offended every deity in existence.

⁙

— TEN —

Despite everything, I had signed a lease for a new apartment down the block. I borrowed money from my credit card for the deposit (swipe, cha-ching, cha-ching), desperate to escape the nightmare of the beachside flea palace. My new place was on the third floor, a cozy studio with cool, refreshing breezes blowing through the windows. Compared to the chaos of the first-floor infestation, it was perfect. It was three blocks from my job waiting tables at the Cheesecake Factory.

With my life running circles around me, I'd become a bit of a poser when it came to surfing. I spent most of my time lounging on my board, feet dangling in the crystal-clear water as I floated around like driftwood. My gaze would settle on the magnificent silhouette of Diamond Head crater, the dormant volcano that towered over the landscape.

A few months had turned into a year, when my little sister Jess stopped in Hawai'i on her way to a summer contract job at a U.S. military base in Japan. Jess had never been to Hawai'i, never seen the ocean. I couldn't wait to show her around the island. She was the only one from Iowa brave enough to visit, and I was determined to make her experience as magical as possible.

There was one tiny detail. Jess still believed that I was, by all accounts, an amazing surfer, and I wasn't about to shatter that illusion. I mean, I had been here for months, so my little sister had every reason to think I had become a pro by now, right?

So, days into her Hawaiian adventure, I decided I would be the one to take her out surfing. Why bother paying for lessons? Lessons were expensive, I had racked up enough debt, and surfing was really a matter of paddling out and popping up on your board at the right time. "Easy," I told myself. "Anyone can do it." And besides, I reasoned, I'd already had my fair share of lessons, and look how far that got me. If I could barely surf after professional instruction, it couldn't be that important.

We made our way to Diamond Head Beach, east of town. It was one of the first places Sven had taken me when I arrived in Honolulu. The place felt familiar, but it had been a while since I'd ventured to this side of the island. But the salty breeze carried the scent of adventure, and I could feel the pressure building. This was my moment to show Jess the ropes, to impress her just like I had impressed my first surf instructor.

Waikiki is usually as tame as a bathtub, with perfect, gentle waves for beginners year-round. That's why I felt so confident about taking Jess out—after all, what could go wrong? What I didn't realize, though, was that the seasons were changing. In O'ahu, the winter months bring monstrous waves to the North Shore, attracting surfers from all over the world. The South Shore, where Waikiki and Diamond Head Beach lie, usually enjoys a much steadier, more relaxed surf. But during this seasonal shift, things can change in ways that even I, with my minimal knowledge of surf reports, hadn't considered.

I hadn't even thought to check the conditions. How bad could it be? It's Waikiki. The surf report probably read something like "easy winds, 3-6 foot waves," which sounded like a breeze. My little sister could handle that. Heck, even if she didn't catch a wave, I figured she could float around and enjoy the jaw-dropping view of Diamond Head, just like I did half the time.

So, brimming with confidence, we descended a steep, well-worn path etched into the side of the mountain. The trail was marked by years of bare feet and sea salt. As we climbed down, pure white sand stretched endlessly along the coast, framed by cliffs dotted with million-dollar homes. It felt like a surf movie, guiding my little sister, the spitting image of Gidget with her two little ponytails, carrying our surfboards through paradise.

We hit the beach and got suited up. I showed Jess how to tether her board to her foot, teaching her whether she should ride goofy-footed or not. I laid her board flat on the sand and coached her through a quick "pop-up" lesson—running her through how to balance, what it feels like when the wave catches you, and the exact moment to rise up and ride. We practiced this for about ten minutes before I sat her down to explain the paddle out, and, most importantly, how her arms would start burning from the effort. "It'll be tough, but you'll get there," I reassured her with all the confidence of someone who, in reality, hadn't braved big waves in months.

With a deep breath, I took the lead and started paddling out toward the waves, checking back every 30 seconds or so to make sure Jess was doing okay. The water looked a little rough, but nothing I hadn't handled before—or so I thought. About two minutes into the paddle, I realized this wasn't going to be as easy as I'd hoped. The waves were rougher than expected, and every stroke felt like I was pushing against a wall of resistance. My arms began to burn, and we hadn't even made it to the lineup yet.

Glancing back at Jess, I saw her determined face bobbing up and down with the waves. She was still hanging in there, paddling like a champ, and even starting to catch up to me. I was proud of her—my baby sister, out here in the big, wide ocean for the first time, keeping pace with me. But beneath that pride, there was a twinge of concern. Something felt off about the waves today. I could sense it in the air, in the way the water pushed against me harder than usual.

As we made our way further out, something became clear—these waves were a lot bigger than I remembered. The sheer size of them was hard to ignore. We finally broke through one of the crests, and I took a moment to show Jess how to keep her board steady in the water. I could tell she was feeling the battle, but when she looked back toward the shore and up to the towering volcano in the distance, her face softened in awe. The view alone made the grueling paddle worth it. I pulled her board closer to mine, pointing out where we were headed next.

"The sea floor's about 80 feet down at this point," I reassured her. "So if you fall off, don't panic. Just fall back, and the leash on your ankle will keep you afloat. The board will always pop back up; just follow the tether back to the surface."

Jess nodded, her face tense with concentration, and asked the question that always lurks in the back of everyone's mind: "What about sharks?"

I laughed, trying to lighten the mood. "Honestly, if a shark showed up right now, paddling back isn't even an option, so you better just catch a wave! Don't try to stand, just lay flat on the board and ride in. It's easy." She smiled, but I could tell there was a flicker of doubt behind her eyes. I pointed out that the waves today were bigger than I'd seen in a while, but I still wasn't overly worried. "Waves come in sets," I explained. "Each one gets progressively bigger, so you have to pay attention. Ride one out, check if more are coming, and don't rush it."

We had about another hundred meters to paddle until we reached the sweet spot, where the waves would really pick up. Jess looked tired, but the adrenaline of being out here was starting to take hold. The view, the waves, and the sheer magnitude of what she was doing had energized her. She looked like she was ready for the challenge. I made a point of reminding her to stay outside of the small group of locals sitting further out, waiting for the next set. "They've been out here for a while," I said. "They know their stuff, but it's all guesswork in the end. We have to sit nearby and be ready when the waves come in."

As we paddled closer, the waves grew more ominous. I could feel the weight of the ocean beneath me in a way I hadn't felt before. These waves weren't just swells—they were like small mountains, rising up out of the sea. I got a knot in my stomach. This wasn't what I had anticipated. "Holy Christ... Oh, Jesus," I muttered under my breath as a massive wave loomed ahead. It was bigger than anything I'd experienced out here. I shot a look back at Jess, who was staring wide-eyed at the colossal wall of water rising before us. She was in awe, probably wondering what the hell I'd gotten her into.

I couldn't help but yell back, "Wait—it gets better!" though, judging by the look on her face, her internal monologue was probably more along the lines of, "What am I doing out here?" Meanwhile, I, her dumb older brother, kept encouraging her to push through, even as my own nerves started to fray. Her arms must've been on fire from the long paddle—mine were too—but this was a whole new level of intensity. The waves were coming in fast, and we were about to be right in the thick of it. Suddenly, I found myself questioning everything. How strong is she? How long can she hold her breath if things go south? I'd traded beginner's water for something much more dangerous.

The waves are rolling in bigger, and my gut is screaming, "Turn back, turn back." But I ignore it—because I'm the big brother, the "pro surfer." Then, Jess yells out over the crashing waves, "Hey, I'm going to turn around!" And every ounce of fake confidence I've been holding onto kicks in. I shout back, "No, no, no! Just one more wave! It's going to be perfect!" But Jess has already made up her mind. She pivots her board, lays down flat, and in an instant, she's out of sight.

Panic surges through me, but there's no time to follow her. I turn back, only to be greeted by the biggest wave I've ever seen in my life. "Holy. Fucking. Shit," is all I can think as this wall of water towers over me, casting a massive shadow that blocks out the sun.

Boom! The wave crashes right on top of me, and I'm instantly ripped from my board, thrown into the churning depths below. The force is unbelievable, like the ocean itself is trying to tear me apart. My body spins uncontrollably, flipping and tumbling through the dark, chaotic water. The world becomes a violent blur of salt and foam. There's no sense of up or down, only the crushing weight of the wave pummeling me deeper. I'm nothing more than a ragdoll in the hands of the ocean.

Then I feel it—the leash attached to my board has wrapped itself around my neck, tightening like a noose. Panic floods my senses as the pull from my board drags me further under. The pressure in my lungs builds, my chest burning as I struggle to keep from inhaling water. The sound of the ocean is deafening, a roaring cacophony that drowns out my frantic thoughts. I'm trapped, unable to break free from the leash that's now suffocating me.

This is it. This is how I die.

I claw desperately at the rope, fingers slipping as the water surges all around me. Every pull feels like I'm fighting against the weight of the entire ocean. My arms are burning, and my mind is spinning in pure survival mode—no rational thought, only desperation. My lungs scream for air as I yank at the cord, feeling it loosen just enough to pull it away from my throat. With one final tug, the rope comes free, and I shoot toward the surface, every muscle in my body straining to get there before it's too late.

I burst through the surface, gasping for air, my lungs heaving, throat raw from the saltwater. The world above is blindingly bright, but I barely have time to adjust before I hear it—the next wave roaring toward me, another massive wall of water. I have no time to react, no time to think.

Boom! The second wave crashes down on me, throwing me right back under, tumbling me like a ragdoll all over again. My limbs are flailing, my body helpless in the chaos. My mind is screaming, "Get up, get up, get up!" but the ocean doesn't care. The force of the water pins me down, swirling in the turbulence. I try to swim, try to find my board, but the water pulls at me like a million invisible hands.

I pop up long enough to take one desperate, gasping breath before the third wave slams into me with all its power. This one feels even heavier, dragging me further under, deeper into the abyss. My chest feels like it's going to burst. The ocean is relentless, uncaring, its weight pressing me down as if it's trying to keep me beneath its surface forever.

Finally, by some miracle, I break through the surface again, choking, gasping for air as I cling to my board. My body is shaking, adrenaline flooding every inch of me. I look around, dazed, searching for something—anything—to anchor me. The waves are still towering, but in the distance, I spot a smaller one, just enough to catch without killing me. Desperate to escape this watery hell, I push toward it, paddling with everything I have left.

I haul myself onto my board, heart racing, still in survival mode. But then it hits me—my little sister is somewhere out here in this chaos. I'm certain she got caught by the wave, totally unprepared for something this brutal. Fear clutches my chest.

"Jess! Jess!" I scream, my voice hoarse. I paddle frantically, scanning the monstrous waves for any sign of her. My heart pounds with every stroke, the terror of what might've happened gripping me harder with each second. Where is she? Is she trapped under a wave, drowning? My mind races with worst-case scenarios, and the uncertainty is paralyzing.

I keep paddling, my arms burning, eyes darting across the horizon. "Jess!" I shout again and again, but there's nothing—no response, no sign of her. I feel like I'm caught in some kind of nightmare, lost in this watery expanse with no clear way out. This is when it hits me: the 10th plague. Pele didn't want my firstborn—she was gunning for my baby sister!

Screaming Jess! Jess! My body is exhausted, I keep pushing through, knowing I have to get back to shore to look for her—or whatever is left of her. Frantically paddling, each wave pushing me closer to the beach, but the panic in my chest only grows. I can't believe this. Where is she? Is she OK? I led her into danger. I'm blind. I can't see anything but the pounding surf, and my mind is a dizzying blur.

And then, finally, as I break through the last of the waves and near the shore, I see her. Sitting on the beach. Calm, collected, and watching me with wide eyes, like, "What the hell is wrong with you?"

I collapse onto the sand, breathless, trembling with relief. Jess looks at me, half-amused, half-terrified. "Dude, what the hell was that? Jesus Christ, are you trying to kill me?"

I lay there in the sand, still catching my breath, barely able to speak. "I'm sorry. I didn't know what the fuck I was doing!"

It was a scene straight out of Joe vs. the Volcano. I was done. Pele had won. She was the Hawaiian goddess of fire, and I—well, I was nothing more than a measly little sacrifice. Her dark tendrils of coiled hair had lashed me for the last time. I got the hint. I burned my eyes into that endless blue sky above Diamond Head crater, drenched and defeated, and shouted, "OKAY, YOU WIN!"

Chapter 7
iCon

Maybe it wasn't Pele who needed to humble me—it was my own need to stop pretending I could conquer every wave, every challenge, just to look like I had it all together. My childhood dreams of amassing a million dollars had obviously drifted far out to sea, but I'd transformed—freedom, adventure, and a life far beyond the cornfields I once called home had shaped me in ways I hadn't anticipated. It wasn't the empire I imagined building as a kid, dreaming of fame and fortune, but it was the escape I'd longed for in those bleak hallways of Holy Ghost school.

Back then, I thought success was measured by how much money you made, how high you could climb. But now, having stumbled across the stages of Broadway, stood beneath the iron turrets of the Eiffel Tower, and basked on the shores of Hawai'i, watching the sunset paint the sky with colors I never could have imagined, I realized life had a different plan for me. I'd traded the corporate ladder for sandy beaches, art shows, and surfboards. Without even knowing it, I'd exchanged dollar signs for experiences that filled my soul rather than my bank account.

And maybe that was the secret I'd been missing all along. Sure, I was poor, but the life I once escaped into through daydreams had finally become my reality—one filled with endless horizons, unexpected opportunities, and the sweet thrill of the unknown that lay just beyond the next flight. It was a vision my dad had instilled in me when he biked across America, and I'd taken that quest for freedom up in my own way.

And just like Moses, I'd finally come to the edge of what seemed like the promised land. Life in Hawai'i calmed down and was shaping up in ways I hadn't expected. My side hustle in photography had become something real. I was shooting weddings, capturing the island's beauty, and working part-time with *Ala Moana* and *Hawaiian Airlines Magazine*, two of Honolulu's top publications. But it was my waitressing gig at the bustling Cheesecake Factory that really raked in the big bucks. Each day, I immersed myself in the world of magazines—working diligently on my computer or skillfully capturing images behind the camera. But as the sun began to set, I'd trade in my creative work for the fast-paced world of waiting tables, catering to the throngs of tourists filling the tiki-lit streets of Waikiki.

I'd arrive at work around 4 p.m., just before the massive dinner rush, and watch as eager tourists lined up down the block, sometimes waiting hours for a table. The Cheesecake Factory was undoubtedly the hotspot of Waikiki, and my ever-growing stash of cash was proof of that. Each night, I'd leave with a hundred or so in tips—it wasn't a fortune, but at least it kept the credit card wolves at bay, letting me make the minimum payments on time.

After my shift ended around 2 a.m., I'd meticulously clean the restaurant, refill ketchup bottles and salt shakers, grab my discounted cheesecake, and start my three-block journey home to my cinder block studio apartment. Each night, as I walked down the still-bustling Waikiki strip, the streets hummed with leftover tourist energy and the neon glow of late-night bars. Around this time, the "glass-slippered" ladies would emerge—the local hookers, defined by their towering clear plastic platform heels, which sparkled under the streetlights like some surreal Cinderella twist.

They lingered at the corners, waiting to pick up their final tricks of the night from the tourists spilling out of bars, eager for one last thrill. I'd walk past them, the weight of a long shift still heavy on my legs, with a pocket full of crumpled dollar bills, cautiously making my way home.

Turning up the dark alley where I lived with a new roommate, the distant hum of Waikiki still in my ears, I was always slightly relieved to make it through those three blocks. The apartment was tiny—barely enough space for the two of us—with a twin-sized mattress and a couch we'd pulled in off the street. Without a Hawaiian bank account, I'd tiptoe to my bed each night, pull out the cash from my pockets, and stuff the crumpled bills under my mattress. In a way, it wasn't riches, but it was fun—a life of making it work, one shift and one dollar at a time.

The money came at a cost. My dedication to paddling out on my board had faded, and between back-to-back day jobs and late-night shifts, my surfboard lay forgotten, collecting dust like a relic of a past life. The nightly indulgences in cheesecake softened the edges of my once-athletic, 20-something surfer body, and the dream of riding the perfect wave had been replaced by the thrill of stashing as much cash as I could under mattresses.

Laura was still running the Starving Artist Award program,

and I decided to throw my hat in the ring for the annual grant they awarded to one artist each year. It was a long shot—I was still in Hawai'i, and the surf and sun felt worlds away from anything so serious.

And in a fortunate twist of fate, I won.

So just as in Exodus, Chapter 20, Verse 12, I was being swept out of the promised land; my Garden of Eden was closing its doors, my days spent lounging on the beach were over. The surfboard, was sold off. It had served its purpose, and now I had to trade the crashing waves for a canvas and a paintbrush once again. I packed up and headed back to New York City, leaving behind the sunsets and warm sands for the cold streets of Manhattan. One day, I was watching the sun dip below the horizon; the next, I was hustling down city sidewalks, diving back into the grind, juggling advertising gigs while working on the grant.

Winning the Starving Artist Award was a turning point. It was just a few thousand dollars, but it was enough to get started. With the grant in hand, I threw myself into my biggest project yet: a series of ten large-scale paintings, each an intense exploration of form and emotion. The pieces were bigger than anything I'd attempted— ten black, apocalyptic 5-foot-by-6-foot canvases. The piece, titled *iCon,* would debut at the Gallery at the Prince George Ballroom in Chelsea, offering a critical look at contemporary American life through the lens of iconic symbols.

This was no small endeavor. *iCon* was a meticulously planned conceptual installation, a real first for me. I wanted to unravel the social fabric of modern American society. The title itself, a play on Apple's ubiquitous branding—like "iPhone" and "iTunes"—hinted at a deeper critique: *i-Con*—the con of consumerism and modern excess. Each of the ten panels was carefully crafted to juxtapose familiar cultural symbols with uncomfortable truths, exposing how these icons mask deeper societal failures. I had come a long way from painting the Eiffel Tower, and maybe the bourgeois were starting to notice.

One side of each pair displayed a haunting rendition of an emblem we all recognize—like the *American Idol* logo placed alongside voter turnout numbers from the show, contrasted with the razor-thin margins of the controversial Bush/Gore election. Another featured a *Freedom to Marry* sticker beside a Bible verse preaching love, pointing out the hypocrisy of using scripture to divide. The images were designed to create an eerie sense of unease, what I described as "scars on the sidewalk after a nuclear attack," leaving behind a subtle yet disturbing imprint.

Another set of panels focused on 9/11, juxtaposing the number of souls lost on that day with the steadily rising death toll of soldiers in the Iraq war, a visual reminder of the human cost that extended far beyond that tragic morning. And the last set was a striking piece where I paired a Louis Vuitton logo with the company's reported profits during the aftermath of Hurricane Katrina, contrasting the billions earned in luxury goods against the comparatively minimal funds allocated for disaster relief—a critique on the lopsided priorities of consumerism and corporate gain over human need.

Standing in the gallery on opening night, surrounded by my own work, I felt like I had finally arrived. This wasn't just an exhibit—it was a conversation about the values we elevate and the sacrifices we ignore. I wasn't just showing art; I was holding up a mirror.

In redefining the American Dream through a lens of consumerism, the work not only confronted the ideals I had once believed in during my youth but also invited viewers to confront an unsettling question: If the symbols of our prosperity—wealth, fame, branding—serve to conceal societal wounds rather than heal them, then what kind of dream are we really chasing? In this reimagining, *iCon* became more than an art piece; it was an invitation to see beyond the glamor of our collective aspirations and question whether the American Dream, in its current form, might indeed be the biggest con of all. For the first time, I could see the impact in people's faces—moments where art shifted from something they looked at to something that looked back at them.

When my parents and Heidi found out I'd won the Starving Artist Award, they didn't waste a second—they planned the trip right away, and even Jill decided to tag along. The last time they'd come to New York was to see *Urinetown* on Broadway, but this trip? This trip was different. This wasn't about the city; it was about me. Everyone dressed to the nines, buzzing with excitement. My mom wore a sleek black-and-white suit with a vibrant red scarf she'd picked out just for the occasion—she looked like a fashion ad. Heidi and Jill? Effortlessly polished, like this wasn't their first New York gallery show (even though it was). Laura stood with them near the entrance, her smile saying it all: she was as proud as if it were her own big night.

I spotted my dad lingering by the gallery door as we finished setting up. His eyes were fixed on the gold letters spelling out my name. He didn't say a word—he didn't need to. He just stood there, hands stuffed in his jacket pockets, staring like he was trying to commit it to memory. From across the room, I watched as he blinked hard, cleared his throat, and stepped inside. It wasn't flashy, it wasn't loud, but it was one of those moments you could feel—pure, quiet pride that hit harder than any big speech ever could.

At the reception, when I took the stage to thank the committee for the award, I shared the story of the Thousand-Armed Goddess of Buddhism—a figure who helps others, with each hand lifting someone in need. "Everyone here," I said, scanning the room, "is one of those hands. You've all helped me succeed."

I started with Jill, who taught me resilience—the ability to adapt and keep going no matter what life throws my way. Then I turned to Heidi, who showed me the power of ambition and adaptability—how to stay graceful under pressure, a lesson I'd seen her master as she played piano and built her career. Next, I thanked my dad, who instilled in me the value of hard work but also the importance of chasing freedom and adventure. Finally, I thanked my mom, who taught me to apply myself and create my own reality, no matter what anyone else said.

Each of them had shaped me in ways I was only beginning to fully appreciate, and standing there in front of that room, having a piece of home with me was poignant—a reminder of the solid foundation of family that made it all possible.

But as fulfilling as the show was, the reality of my daily life pulled me back to earth. Awards and art shows didn't pay all the bills; they were helping me build a balance, but I still needed a steady income. And so, a few weeks later, I drifted back to my day job, blissfully unaware that I was walking into one of the strangest—and most painful—episodes of my life. It started like any other morning, but I was excited—Subway had just launched a line of low-calorie breakfast sandwiches! I grabbed an egg white sandwich with turkey bacon, fully convinced it would help me shed those stubborn pounds I'd gained from too many late-night, half-priced Cheesecake Factory slices on the streets of Waikiki.

By lunchtime, things took a nosedive. I felt anything but great—what I could only assume was food poisoning, courtesy of Subway. Everyone assumed I was being my best dramatic self, calling on my theater skills, but this time, something was really wrong. After a few agonizing hours curled up on the mailroom floor, I finally told my boss I was heading home, barely able to stay upright on the subway.

I staggered into my apartment, texted my friends Kim and Laura, and decided, *eh*, maybe the ER is a good idea. We arranged to meet at St. Vincent's. By the time I got there, I could barely stand, and even the triage nurse could see I was in bad shape. But as fate would have it, the hospital was closing for good that very day— about to be remade into condos—and they didn't want to admit me. Doubled over in pain, they finally let me in anyway.

Kim was filling out paperwork, while they pumped me full of morphine as I lay writhing on the ER bed, feeling like I was giving birth to some hideous half-human, half-vampire creature from *Eclipse*, tearing me up from the inside. In my haze, I thought, *Edward Cullen, how could you do this to me!* Flickers of faces and lights hovered above me—the doctors, the bright lights, and then finally, surgery. Appendicitis.

A few days later, the hospital began closing its inpatient recovery rooms and releasing patients to go home. Though I was still in pain after they removed the wretched beast from my abdomen, my doctor cleared me for discharge. But only days after getting home, I found myself back in his office, the space filled with stacks of boxes as he prepared to move out with the rest of the closing hospital staff.

As he examined me, the doctor's face grew serious. It turned out my appendix had burst during surgery, and though they'd tried to clean everything up, a massive infection had been brewing in my stomach. *Jesus*, that stubborn vampire baby just wouldn't go away. It was a dumb premise for a book; it was a worse premise for real life.

They needed a CAT scan to confirm if the infection had indeed grown another head, but with the hospital closed, there were no paramedics. So, I headed outside toward NY Downtown Hospital just south of Chinatown. With no cabs in sight and only an express train departing, I fumbled down the subway steps, hunched over in pain, and caught the 2 train to Fulton Street.

When I finally got there, even though they were expecting me, there was a long stretch of waiting—first for a stretcher, then in a hallway, and finally for the CAT scan. They handed me a bottle of the foulest-tasting liquid I'd ever had to drink so they could get a clearer view, and I choked it down, hoping this would all be over soon.

They laid me on the CAT scan table, and as the scan started, I noticed the technician's face growing serious. They scanned me once, twice, and then called more doctors into the room. That's when I knew this wasn't good.

One of the doctors approached and said, "There's a large abscess. We can't risk moving you to the OR, so we'll need to operate right here on the CAT scan table."

So, right there, with me half-dazed from pain, they prepped and began the procedure. I stared up at the intense lights, overcome by the surreal feeling of being operated on in the scanning room. Everything felt like a scene from *Grey's Anatomy*, except it was my body on the table, and there was no McDreamy in sight.

I was in a hospital bed when I woke up, with a drainage bag taped to my side. And after another seven days in the hospital, I was discharged with a delightful infection-draining bag that became my constant companion. I even showed up at Laura's birthday party with the drain hanging out of my jeans, much to everyone's horror.

I had racked up tens of thousands in medical debt without insurance, effectively zeroing out any pursuit of riches in my near future. And it was 2008, just weeks after the financial crisis had hit Manhattan like a wrecking ball. My mom, stressed out over how

I'd pay these bills—now double my college loans—along with my growing credit card debt (cha-ching), saw the cash register total become insurmountable. One night, she was up late watching Suze Orman. With the world in shambles, Suze suggested people consider bankruptcy as if she were advising on a new savings plan. My mom, taking Suze to heart, found me a lawyer, and we embarked on the endless paperwork and filings that bankruptcy required. I mean, everyone was doing it back then; it was practically a trend—bleak, but in fashion.

Somehow, I found myself shifting from scheming to get rich... to desperately trying to get debt-free—and I have to admit, it was a little devastating. It felt like admitting defeat, as though all my hustling and adventures had led me straight into a pit of despair. I hadn't realized just how fragile my situation was—one hospital visit away from crushing financial ruin. Filing for bankruptcy was its own ordeal, a hassle of endless meetings, notaries at every corner, and dizzying legal jargon. On top of that, the weeks I'd spent in the hospital had upended my prospects entirely—my freelance gigs had dried up, leaving me unemployed and charging rent to my credit cards (cha-ching, cha-ching, cha-ching). Had I been delusional this whole time? Maybe I wasn't a dreamer; maybe I was just reckless.

Clawing my way out of that financial pit felt like using a plastic spoon to scale a mountain. Thankfully, unemployment kept me afloat while I filed for bankruptcy, and small gigs started trickling in. Shooting weddings in the Catskills on weekends didn't fix everything, but at least it put groceries on the table and gave me the faintest glimmer of hope that I could rebuild from scratch.

When I showed up to court for my hearing, I felt embarrassed, like a failure, and, most of all, ridiculous. There I was, saddled with a few thousand dollars in debt from medical bills, rent, and years of random credit card charges (cha-ching), while the guy next to me was scrambling to keep his Ferrari, Hamptons home, and high-rise apartment. The Monopoly Man sure has a funny way with life. The judge basically looked at me and laughed, stamped "approved" like I was a shoo-in for the minor leagues, and sent me on my way.

The rules were simple: no debt, no credit cards, no passing go and collecting $200. Just good old-fashioned cash for seven years. It wasn't too bad; most days, I made it work, though every now and then, I'd give my mom a call with my best "Hey, remember your favorite child?" voice to help cover the rent.

Chapter 8
The Candlestick Maker

For the first time since I'd hopped off the bus at Port Authority, I was finally debt-free. Within a few months, I landed a cool job at a digital advertising school, doing marketing and graphic design for a Swedish company just starting up in America. It had promise. So, with the constant need for money and stability still pushing me forward, like the American workhorse I was always told I was supposed to be, I hopped on and settled in for the ride—now that I was financially sound, I could feel that hope for the ever-elusive million-dollar dream starting to crest the horizon.

Yet, romance has its own way of diverting a person. I started dating a charming boy named Ethan, born in Indonesia, with a slim frame, beautiful almond eyes, and a preppy little haircut that made him stand out in any room. His family had moved to Flushing, Queens, when he was young, and he carried a captivating blend of old-world charm and city grit. As the oldest of two boys, he went by his Indonesian name, "Adi," at home. I recognized something in him that felt familiar—the same scheming and dreaming energy I had as a child.

Ethan lived in the dorms at the New Yorker Hotel on 34th Street, and our dates often revolved around catching movies and grabbing food at the Tick-Tock Diner. That place became *our spot*— though in reality, it was more mine than his, considering I carried around an extra 10 pounds from eating tons of chocolate chip pancakes there.

In some ways, food was the thing that truly connected us. Ethan was obsessed with cake. We would trek across Koreatown, Chinatown, and Flushing, chasing down the best desserts, as if it were the glue holding our very different worlds together. There was a science to baking that he loved, something that reflected his logical mind.

Ethan, who aspired to be a forensic detective, would often talk about feelings and emotions as if they were scientific concepts— breaking them down like formulas, something that made perfect sense to him but left me utterly baffled.

"You know," he said one evening, leaning back on his dorm bed, watching an episode of *Bones* "people's reactions are like chemical reactions. Add the right catalyst, and boom—explosion."

I raised an eyebrow. "Are you saying you can predict emotions like equations?"

"Pretty much," he said with a grin. "Like you, for instance. You're the type who... needs coffee as a buffer before anyone talks to you in the morning. Classic reaction."

"Okay, Sherlock," I laughed, "maybe it's just that I don't like mornings."

"No, see, that's the formula!" he insisted, his eyes alight with that intense curiosity. "Everyone's got one. And if I ever figure it out, maybe I'll solve the mysteries of the universe... or at least the mystery of you." He nudged me, softly laughing to himself.

In that banter, we found a kind of comfort. He had served in the

Navy before college, stationed in the Middle East, which helped him attend school on the G.I. Bill. It gave him a bit of worldliness, but I still saw that same dreamer's naivety in him—the kind that made me feel oddly protective. He was always tossing around grand ideas, and every conversation felt like staring at a blank canvas full of potential. I wanted to shield him from the missteps and pitfalls I knew too well, to guide him through the challenges I had already faced.

One of his deepest passions was baking—cakes, pastries, candies—you name it, he loved it. It reminded me of those Saturday afternoons spent with Jess and my mom, frosting hundreds of my grandmother's sugar cookies. Baking was a family tradition, and it always felt like a way of bringing us closer. For Ethan, it was the same. We were always mixing up a batch of chocolate-covered strawberries or a chocolate soufflé—*he* was the scientist, not me; my soufflé always flopped. Even while attending school, he found a way to turn his love for sweets into something tangible. He opened an Etsy shop—not just any shop, but one that perfectly reflected his personality. He crafted soy candles that smelled like crème brûlée, a nod to his baking skills.

"You ever think of opening a café?" he asked, out of nowhere one day, as we were looking for cake in Koreatown. "Or, I don't know, starting a business?"

"Opening a café?" I laughed. "I thought about it as a kid. But you're the one with a million business ideas. Me? I'd probably just decorate the place in rainbows and never make a buck."

He nudged me with his elbow. "Well, when you're ready, I'll be there to bail you out. Every business needs a dreamer and a realist."

And in that moment, my face softened. "You're the realist, huh?"

He looked away, smiling. "Guess I am."

In those moments, I saw both the innocence and passion in

him, the same things I had wrestled with for years. I cared about him deeply, not just for who he was but for the potential I saw in him—his mix of dreams and determination reminded me so much of myself.

We spent hours bringing his candle shop vision to life. I helped him design the logo—an elegant lotus flower with a flame at its center, inspired by Buddha's teachings. It was the perfect symbol for Ethan: a balance of calm, creativity, and burning ambition. The shop gave him purpose, a way to bring joy and warmth into people's homes, as he'd once dreamed of doing with his café. Each candle he made felt like a step toward that dream, and I was proud to stand by his side, helping him make it a reality.

We dated for a year, and while our romantic relationship eventually came to an end, he remained my best friend. Ethan was someone I cared for deeply, and I wanted to make sure he never lost that spark. We met up regularly—dinners over Korean BBQ, sunny afternoons giggling over bubble tea in Chinatown. He was the kind of person you could count on: kind, curious, and unwaveringly hopeful. There was a quiet strength in him, a way of seeing the world that made you want to believe in better things. Being around Ethan made me want to be better, too.

A week before I left for Paris for work, Ethan and I grabbed pad thai at Max's restaurant—his new boyfriend's place. The warm aroma of peanuts and lime filled the air, a comforting scent that matched Ethan's easygoing nature. We ate and laughed, talking about everything and nothing, like we always did. It was one of those moments where time folded in on itself—no matter how much had changed, we still slipped effortlessly into the same rhythm. I felt deeply grateful for him, for the way he steadied me in a world that often felt too chaotic.

"You're crushing it," Ethan said, grinning between bites of

noodles. "Paris, million-dollar events, speaking French like you've been doing it forever. What's next? Hosting the Emmys?"

I smirked, swirling my fork through the pad thai. "Oh, please. I'm just trying to keep the wheels turning. You're the one with the new boyfriend, new life. Look at you."

"Max is sweet," he said, his tone softening. "But let's not make this about me. This isn't the Ethan show—it's your moment, Luke. You're finally in your element."

"Maybe," I said, shrugging. "But you know me—I'm always chasing something. Not just work, but... I don't know. Something more. Something real."

Ethan leaned back, studying me the way he always did when he knew I was deflecting. "You'll find it," he said quietly. "You've already got more magic in you than most people could dream of."

I laughed it off, but his words stayed with me. They always did. Ethan had this way of seeing me clearer than I saw myself.

By then, I had transitioned into a new phase of my career, pulling off one of my biggest achievements yet: a million-dollar event for top advertising agencies in Paris. It was a huge milestone. Standing before the audience, I delivered the entire introduction in French, earning laughs when I credited my language skills to watching dubbed Disney movies and devouring every translated Harry Potter book I could get my hands on. Their laughter filled the room, and for a brief moment, I felt unstoppable, like I belonged in this dazzling world of champagne receptions and high-stakes ideas. It had been 10 years since I'd last wandered these streets, but the magic of Paris hadn't faded—it was as if the city was welcoming me back with open arms.

But amid that professional high, I got the text...

"Luke, the paramedics are here," Max wrote. "Ethan's sick, but they don't think it's pneumonia because his lungs didn't crackle."

I reread the message, my stomach twisting. The fact that they had called paramedics at all hit me like a jolt. I couldn't shake the dread rising in me. The words blurred as I read them again and again, trying to make sense of it. Despite the distance, I felt an overwhelming need to be there for him, as I always had. Ethan had been my anchor, and now I needed to find a way to be his.

When I landed back in New York, the weight of Ethan's situation hit me immediately. His condition had worsened, and while Max was doing his best, it was clear they were in over their heads. Of course, I stepped in. It wasn't even a question—I'd always been his protector.

Within hours of stepping off the plane, I knew this was way beyond home remedies or a casual doctor's visit. He'd been misdiagnosed with bronchitis, and that little mistake had made everything spiral. I called for an ambulance, and when the paramedics arrived, the look on their faces said everything I didn't want to admit—this was serious.

As they lifted him onto the stretcher and carried him down the four flights of stairs, I followed, my stomach in knots. Each step felt like a lifetime. Every little jolt seemed to rattle him more, and I was helpless, watching it all unfold like some slow-motion nightmare.

When we got outside, the flashing lights from the ambulance lit up the street, casting shadows that made everything feel even more surreal. I climbed into the back, sitting next to Ethan, who was barely hanging on, his breathing shallow and strained. The sound of the sirens was a strange comfort, even as the weight of the situation pressed down harder on me with every passing minute.

By the time we arrived at the hospital, they had already decided to sedate and intubate him. I didn't know much about medical procedures, but the sight of them preparing him for the ventilator shook me. His lungs were full of fluid, and it was clear he couldn't breathe on his own. I held Ethan's hand, and he scribbled notes on scraps of paper, apologizing for not being able to speak, his exhaustion evident in every shaky word.

Once Ethan was intubated, his body's stats were all over the place. His breathing grew labored, and his heart rate would skyrocket—sometimes reaching over 170 beats per minute. Max and I could only sit there in horror, helpless as we watched the monitors blink and beep. We had no idea what was truly happening inside his body, and the doctors weren't forthcoming with clear answers. All we knew was that he had two different types of pneumonia, yet no one could fully understand what was going on, leaving us lost in the uncertainty of his condition. We just had to wait, agonizing over every number on those screens.

At just twenty-seven, Ethan's life hung in a fragile balance. His boyfriend, Max, and I were consumed with anxiety, not knowing how to process the tragedy unfolding before our eyes. We hesitated to call his mother, afraid to burden her with the weight of what was happening. But as the night dragged on, and Ethan's condition worsened, we knew there was no choice.

Pacing the sterile hospital hallways, I gripped a Styrofoam cup of lukewarm coffee, the only comfort in sight. Max looked at me, his eyes red and exhausted.

"Are you going to call her, or should I?" he asked, his voice cracking.

I took a breath, nodding. "I'll do it."

When his mother answered, I could hear the tremble in her voice as I explained her son's condition—that Ethan was in a hospital bed, hooked to a ventilator, fighting for his life.

She was quiet, her words whispered, and telling her broke my heart all over again.

After hanging up, we sat together, bracing for her arrival. In the haze that followed came a barrage of paperwork. I was the one filling out forms, answering questions, and signing as his emergency contact. Max and Ethan's mother, both overwhelmed and limited by language barriers, looked to me to handle the logistics and translate as best as I could.

Max shook his head, his voice barely a whisper. "I don't know what we'd do if you hadn't come back in time."

"I should've been here earlier," I replied, glancing around the bustling hospital, feeling the weight of responsibility. "I just hope we got here early enough."

This was before the Affordable Care Act, and his veteran's insurance from his service in the Navy had lapsed—another layer of complication we didn't need. That's why he hadn't come to the hospital sooner; he was too afraid of the costs. The hospital buzzed around me with its fluorescent lights and efficient movements, yet I stood there in the middle of it all, feeling like I was watching someone else's life unfold.

The doctors explained it would be better to place Ethan in a medically induced coma. His lungs, now ravaged by double pneumonia, could no longer sustain him without help. He lay still, surrounded by beeping machines and the sterile coldness of hospital sheets. Max and I never left his side, day and night blending into a blur of cold hospital rooms and whispered conversations. I remember the sound of the ventilator, its steady rhythm becoming the cruel soundtrack to those unbearable weeks.

The Upper West Side hospital room became our second home. The chairs were stiff, the air conditioning relentless—so much so that I would wrap myself in whatever coat or blanket I could find, trying to keep warm during those bone-chilling nights. Max, Ethan's mother, and I took turns sitting at his bedside, holding his hand, speaking to him in hopes he could still hear us. But most of the time, all I could do was watch him lie there, fighting, and feel utterly helpless. There were moments when the weight of it all was so overwhelming that I'd step outside, the cold New York air biting at my skin, just to breathe, to pray, to question how we had gotten here.

Around Thanksgiving, we nearly lost him. One night, the doctor came into the room where Max, Ethan's family, and I were sitting. His face said it all. "It doesn't look good," he told us, bracing us for the worst. That night, while trying to sleep, I couldn't stop the relentless thoughts—if only we had caught it earlier, before I'd returned from Paris, could it have made a difference? Could we have saved him before the pneumonia spread and took hold? Guilt gnawed at me, and I would have done anything—given anything—to turn back time. But all I could do now was sit beside him, gripping his hand, praying with more desperation than I'd ever prayed in my life. I prayed to every god, every spirit, anything that could hear me. And miraculously, Ethan began to stabilize. And after what felt like an eternity, the doctors brought him out of the coma in early December. He wasn't out of the woods, but for the first time, there was hope.

We spent all of Christmas by his bedside. Ethan was doing better. The doctors eventually removed the tube from his throat and inserted a smaller one into his neck. There was a palpable sense of relief in the air, a glimmer of hope that things were finally turning around. Jess was getting married in Peru over New Year's, and as Ethan's condition improved, I felt confident enough to travel.

At the wedding, I shared photos with him over Facebook, each snapshot capturing us dressed in our fanciest clothes, smiling through the whirlwind of love and celebration. Ethan, ever the cheerleader, liked and commented on every post. "Looking sharp!" he wrote under one picture, and even his mom chimed in, sending her love. Even from thousands of miles away, Ethan felt present—his words a lifeline of humor and encouragement that kept us connected. These little digital exchanges, though small, were meaningful reminders of his strength and the community rallying around him.

When I returned from Peru, Ethan looked great—still skinny, still weak—but alive. It felt like we were finally reaching the light at the end of a very long tunnel. Over the months, I had been working from the hospital while he lay in a coma, but things were better now. Setting up my laptop next to his bed while he watched TV felt like a small triumph in itself—a sign of progress. I was there the day they put the speaking valve on his tube, a moment that felt like another victory. Ethan, in true form, used his first words to ask for congee— his favorite warm, comforting rice soup. Even in his most fragile moments, food was always on his mind, and that small, familiar request felt like a win—a glimpse of the Ethan we all knew and loved.

As things continued to improve, I spent less time at the hospital, reassured that Ethan's mom was there more often. My boss, however, was another source of stress entirely. Still, February brought a long-awaited milestone: after nearly five months in and out of the ICU, Ethan was discharged. The joy of that moment was overwhelming, like we'd climbed a mountain and could finally see the view.

I helped Max move their apartment from 54th Street to a new place above Ethan's mom's in Flushing, Queens. On a frigid January day, five of us crammed into the back of a moving truck, shivering in the darkness as we rode along the BQE. The move had been thrown together with a ragtag crew and some Chinese movers who charged next to nothing—a few hundred dollars—but it felt like a small victory. Ethan was back where he belonged, closer to family, and surrounded by people who would ensure he had the support he needed to keep moving forward.

By mid-February, Ethan was home, right in time for Valentine's Day. True to form, he asked me to bring him cake from the French pastry shop behind my apartment. It was the kind of request that made me smile, even in the middle of all the chaos, because Ethan never let his love for cake fade, no matter how sick he was. But instead of just cake, I decided to go all out and picked up a bucket of KFC too—his favorite—and brought it over to his new place. We sat in his living room, sharing greasy fried chicken with his mom and his aunt. The mood was lighter than it had been in months, and for that one night, it felt like we could all pretend things were normal. Max was at work, but Ethan, his mom, and I laughed, talked, and ate together, grateful for the brief moment of peace.

Within weeks of being home, Ethan's condition took a sudden turn for the worse. The cold, damp weather seemed to seep into his bones, dragging him back into the illness even faster than before. It all happened so quickly, we barely had time to react—one moment he was resting, trying to recover, and the next, he was rushed back to the hospital. This time, though, it felt different. The fight was slipping away from him, and we all knew it, even if we couldn't bring ourselves to say it out loud.

That night, I went home feeling so sick I could barely move. The weight of everything, the helplessness—it was crushing. I spent the night tossing and turning, trying to fight back the nausea and the aching in my chest. In the early hours of the morning, a text came. "Come to the hospital." I didn't hesitate. I ran as fast as I could, but deep down, I knew.

Panicked, I grabbed a cab from Wall Street to Flushing. When I arrived at the hospital, the gravity of the situation hit me hard. Ethan was so sick, this time quarantined, and the tubes were back in place. His mom, clearly overwhelmed, asked me to speak to the doctor and find out what was really going on. I pulled the doctor aside and told him that Ethan's mother didn't understand what was happening. The doctor looked me dead in the eye, right in front of Ethan and his mom, and said, "He's not going to make it through the night."

I froze. "Does Ethan know?" I asked, barely able to get the words out. The doctor nodded. "Yes, he knows. We've told him." I felt like the air had been sucked out of the room. I couldn't believe it. "He was just fine a week ago!" I protested, my voice breaking. "But he was doing better!" I was desperate, begging the doctor for options. "Can't we do a lung transplant? Change hospitals? Can't we try something else?" But he repeated what he had said. There was nothing more they could do.

Tears already stinging my eyes, I explained to Max and his mom what the doctor had been saying. We all broke down, crying together. It didn't feel real. None of us expected this. It was like a nightmare we couldn't wake up from.

We stayed with Ethan through the night, texting friends to come and say goodbye. People trickled in, all as stunned as we were. I took Ethan's hand, holding it tight. I leaned down and told him, "I love you. I hope you know that." He nodded weakly, and I squeezed his hand as hard as I could, willing this all to stop.

On the morning of April 4th, 2012, six months after I returned to New York, at just 27 years old, Ethan lost his battle. The memory of that moment is burned into me with painful clarity. The hospital room felt too still, the machines were quiet, and the coldness of the room pressed down on me like a suffocating blanket. He was gone. And with him, the light and laughter he brought into my life. The weight of it all came crashing down, and for the first time, I couldn't stop the tears. I had lost my friend, my anchor, and the realization left me utterly powerless.

The next few days were a blur. I couldn't eat, couldn't drink, couldn't do anything. I lost 10 pounds in less than two weeks, my body reflecting the grief that had consumed me. I was so distraught I ended up at the clinic. I couldn't swallow food; I couldn't even drink water. The stress had ravaged my body, burning my esophagus to the point where I was unable to ingest anything. As I sat in the hospital, sucking on ice cubes to get water, the world spun around me. Everything felt disjointed, like I was stuck in a nightmare I couldn't wake up from.

I was placed on a high dose of antacids and given an IV to manage the physical toll the grief had taken on my body. But no medication could touch the weight that settled deep within me. Losing Ethan was like losing a part of my own heart. He was the first person so young and close to me that I had ever lost, and the shock of it reverberates through my life to this day. There seemed to be no reason for him to die. He was full of life, full of dreams—someone who should have had years ahead of him.

At the funeral, Kim, my college friend who had helped me land that job on Broadway, and has been ever the steady presence in my life, stood by my side in my fragile state. I was asked to be a pallbearer, lifting Ethan's casket on a bitterly cold day in Flushing. The air was sharp, and every breath felt like it weighed a thousand pounds. As we carried him to his final resting place, the sun—almost mocking in its brightness—filtered through the bare trees, casting long shadows across the ground. It felt surreal, like the world had no business being beautiful on a day that felt so broken.

He had been a mystery to me in so many ways, his mind always spinning with equations, concepts, and ideas that left me bewildered but admiring. And yet, despite our differences, we had shared something unspoken—a bond forged in late-night talks and the simple joy of seeking out the best slice of cake in the city. I thought about how we had laughed, debated, and found joy in those small moments, moments that now felt like tiny treasures, more valuable than I had ever realized.

As I gripped the handles of his casket, I felt the weight not only of his body but of all the memories, the unsaid words, the unresolved emotions. The things I never got to ask him, the things he never had a chance to say.

The ceremony was a traditional Buddhist wake, and it felt strange, foreign, and overwhelming. There was a lot of chanting and bowing—loud, ritualistic cries that filled the air for nearly an hour. They put two coins over his eyes and a pearl in his mouth to shepherd him on his journey. A pearl, believed to have the ability to protect him, to ensure a smooth journey through the underworld. The coins on his eyes were for paying guardian spirits so that he would have a safe passage. I participated in a walking chant around Ethan's casket and his photo, but I was so sick that I nearly tripped over the photo stand, almost knocking the incense over. It was a blur, the whole thing—a surreal, heartbreaking blur.

We left Flushing and made the long drive to Calverton National Cemetery, the military burial ground in Long Island, the final resting place for those who had served their country. Ethan's casket was draped in the crisp, solemn folds of the American flag—a symbol of his time in the Navy. As the soldiers began their slow, deliberate movements, folding the flag with military precision, the weight of the moment became almost unbearable. Each fold seemed to echo the finality of it all. When they finished, they handed the neatly folded flag to Ethan's mother, their voices low and respectful as they thanked her for her son's service to our country.

The trumpets played "Amazing Grace," the mournful notes cutting through the stillness of the day. It was a beautiful, almost surreal contrast—the sun shining brightly through the bare trees of the cemetery, while we all stood there, struggling to reconcile the cold reality of the moment. Ethan was gone, but in that solemn tribute, it felt like a piece of him remained, honored and remembered by the country he had served.

And as the final words were spoken and the casket lowered into the ground, I thought of all the cakes he would never get to bake, the scientific discoveries he would never make, and the conversations we would never have. He was gone, and yet, in my heart, he still coursed through me.

In the weeks that followed, hospital bill collectors began calling—I had signed all the paperwork when he was unconscious, now hundreds of thousands of dollars in bills had come due. I'd throw down the phone crying and yell, "He's dead!" before hanging up. Hadn't I just gone through this in my own life? I stopped answering, and eventually, they stopped calling.

Through the heartache, I began to grasp how fragile life really is. I learned that the moments we share with our loved ones are more precious than we often realize, and Ethan's vibrant spirit became a reminder to live fully, because we never know how much time we have. His memory stayed with me, a guiding force pushing me to find meaning in the aftermath of such a profound loss. Ethan was bound to the heavens, and I was tethered to the earth—like the two halves of the Naupaka flower I had once found on the jagged rock shores of Hawai'i, forever separated, never to be whole again.

Ethan's passing left a deep hole in my life, and I found myself searching for a way to honor him in a tangible, meaningful way. We had shared a connection to Buddhism—not that I was particularly religious—but he took me to the temple in Chinatown for the first time. Somehow, I had never known it was there. He taught me about the zodiac, its symbolism and meaning, and even bought me a small wooden charm that I still carry with me. It was on that day that we came up with the idea for his candle logo. And that's when my mind returned to the candles—his candles.

One day, after months of being lost, I decided to visit his family in Flushing, feeling a deep pull to reconnect with Ethan's world.

As I walked through the familiar streets of his neighborhood, I was overwhelmed by memories of him that still lingered in every corner. The mall where we'd wandered together aimlessly, the Korean BBQ spot where we shared meals and stories, and the bucket of KFC chicken we brought him when he finally got out of the hospital. Everywhere I looked, it felt like Ethan was still there, in the small, everyday moments we had shared.

When I arrived at his mother's house, I knew what I had to ask, but the words felt heavy. I sat down with her, knowing this was about more than candles—it was about turning all the sorrow into something meaningful. I told her I wanted to borrow Ethan's candle supplies—the molds, the wicks, the scents—so I could make candles in his honor, continuing the craft he had poured so much love into. His candles had been more than a hobby; they were a piece of his heart, filled with warmth and creativity. I hoped that by carrying on this part of his dream, I could channel my grief into something positive, something that kept his light alive.

She smiled warmly and said she would love that.

So, I took Ethan's supplies back to my place, and it felt like I was carrying a part of him with me. I set up a small space in my apartment and started making candles—blending the scents I had carefully chosen, remembering how much joy and passion he had put into his work. It became more than just making candles; it was a way to keep his spirit alive, to share his light with others in a way that felt intimate and real. Each candle I poured felt like a piece of Ethan, glowing brightly—a reminder that even though he was gone, the warmth he brought into the world could still be felt.

After visiting his mother's house, I threw myself into the task of figuring out how best to honor Ethan. I spent weeks learning the art of candle-making, determined to recreate the essence of the candles he once crafted. I redesigned his lotus flower logo, and beneath it, in elegant script, I named the collection "Adi" after his Indonesian name, which means "superior" and is traditionally bestowed upon the firstborn.

The scents that had always filled his apartment now filled mine as I worked late into the night, experimenting with wax, wicks, and fragrances. It became more than a creative outlet—it was a way to keep him close, to turn my grief into something tangible and meaningful. But I knew I wanted to do more than make candles. I wanted to create something that would allow others to honor their loved ones too, just as I was honoring Ethan.

That's when the idea for My Light Shines was born. I embarked on a crowdfunding campaign with the goal of distributing candles worldwide, each one dedicated to someone who had passed. Every candle would come with a code that could be entered on the website I was building, allowing people to light their candle online and leave a tribute. It was a way to create something lasting—something that connected people through their shared experiences of loss. After filming a heartfelt video and pouring my soul into the campaign, to my astonishment, we sold hundreds of candles in over forty countries.

But fulfilling the promises of a crowdfunding campaign isn't easy. I found myself in my New York City apartment, surrounded by wax, wicks, boxes, and orders I needed to fulfill. I had promised to get everything shipped out before the anniversary of Ethan's death, and the pressure was on. I was still perfecting my candle-making skills, learning how to melt the wax just right, how to balance the scents, and how to avoid spills—all while running the website.

One winter night, as the deadline loomed, Laura came over to help me. I was behind schedule, stressed, and exhausted. In an attempt to unwind, we cracked open a bottle of wine. But in our distraction, I accidentally overheated the wax and burned the entire first batch of candles. In a panic, I tried to salvage what I could and ended up pouring the ruined wax down the toilet—only to have it immediately solidify, turning my toilet into a giant candle.

It was absolutely freezing in New York, and the building's ancient plumbing was no match for the disaster I'd created. The toilet was clogged with solid wax, completely jammed up beyond repair. I frantically called a plumber, only to be told they couldn't come until the next day. Panic set in—how was I going to fix this? That's when Laura and I turned to the one lifeline we had left: YouTube. To my surprise, I wasn't the first person to do this—there were actual tutorials on how to unclog a toilet filled with wax.

Armed with a ridiculous level of determination and some boiling pots of water, we set out to melt the wax and flush it down the toilet in a last-ditch effort to save the night. Every time we poured in a new pot, we'd watch with bated breath as steam billowed up, hoping the wax would finally dislodge. It was both ridiculous and desperate— Laura and I laughing through the absurdity of it all, while knowing we were one step away from making things so much worse.

Despite the chaos, the campaign was ultimately a success. I had a monk come over and bless the candles in remembrance of Ethan's spirit. As all the candles found their boxes and went out into the world, the map on My Light Shines (www.mylightshines.com) filled up with pins from all over the globe, each one representing a dedication to someone's lost loved one. It became a beautiful statement to the connections we share through our grief.

Through all the missteps, the lessons in candle-making, and even the toilet fiasco, I learned the value of perseverance. It wasn't only about honoring Ethan anymore; it was about pushing forward through every obstacle, knowing that he would be proud of what we'd created together. The campaign and the website stood as an ephemeral testament to the power of love and community, proof that even in the darkest moments, something beautiful can emerge.

In the end, I like to imagine Ethan looking down at me, laughing as I boiled water to fix the wax-filled toilet. He'd probably say, "Of course you turned this into an adventure." And in many ways, I did—just like we always did together.

Ethan Adi Guidjaja

April 19th, 1984 - April 4th, 2012

Chapter 9
Zen Master

After Ethan left me, it took a long time to find peace. The grief was raw, and for years, I blamed myself, convinced I should have been able to save him. It was like the constant beat of a drum: If you had been there. If we hadn't let him go home. If... If... If. I started running—5k, 10k, and beyond—pushing myself as if each step could leave the pain behind. But the truth is, I wasn't just running for fitness or escape. I was running from myself, from the grind, from the relentless ache of not knowing what I was searching for—or if I'd even know it when I found it. What was I running toward? Peace? Purpose? Forgiveness? I didn't have the answers, but I couldn't stop chasing them.

I lost my job—I just couldn't hold it together. But I was still in New York full-time and found work freelancing as a designer for pharmaceuticals. The money was there, but the spark wasn't. I was starting to feel like I'd never, in my whole life, found myself anywhere but restless and discontent—especially in this city, as the winter chill seemed to seep into my bones. One freezing January day, I'd had enough. I grabbed my backpack, and once again, I took off. I needed out—I was a mess and needed a way to find peace. But why did peace always feel like it was somewhere else, never here? The allure of Asia and its spirituality was calling me.

You know how movies like *Eat, Pray, Love* got all the millennials obsessed with soul-searching? Well, I wasn't going to miss out. And if that lady made a million dollars off her story, I figured my chances were at least 50/50. I downloaded the Headspace app, threw myself into meditating every day, and thought, "If I can gamify being Zen, I'm going to master it!"

Bangkok was just a pit stop on the way to my real destination. The airport buzzed with its usual chaos—streams of people rushing in every direction, the humid air slamming into me the second I stepped outside. But that's a story for another day. Right now, I had a commuter flight to catch to Laos.

As we descended from 30,000 feet, the view took my breath away. The landscape below was nothing short of extraordinary. Lush, emerald-green mountains stretched as far as the eye could see, their jagged peaks swathed in mist. Winding rivers cut through the valley like muddy ribbons, shimmering under the tropical sun. Dense forests blanketed the land, their vibrant hues almost too rich to believe, with hints of lush rice paddies tucked into the hillsides. It was a far cry from the urban sprawl and noise of the cities I knew. Instead, this was a world of untamed beauty—a landscape that seemed to pulse with a different kind of life. The sprawling river valleys were wide and serene, dotted with small wooden homes and farmland, where clusters of palm trees swayed gently in the warm breeze. Everything felt alive, from the vivid greens of the foliage to the sparkling waters that reflected the clear sky.

When we touched down at the tiny airport in Luang Prabang, the contrast was stark. The airport was humble and quiet, a far cry from Bangkok's sprawling chaos. But even in this small, unassuming place, the sense of adventure was palpable. I exited the airport into a dusty parking lot filled with taxis, feeling the weight of the humid air settle over me. It was then that a tall Canadian guy, looking as bewildered as I did, tapped me on the shoulder and asked, "Wanna split a cab?"

With a budget traveler's mindset, I immediately agreed. Anyone looking to save a few bucks on the ride into town was fine by me. And with Laos unfolding before me, every moment felt like the start of something incredible.

We climbed into a beat-up cab with seats worn thin from countless passengers. The driver barely spoke English but nodded when we showed him the address. As we bumped along the uneven roads, the Canadian and I got to talking. He had visited some friends in Hong Kong and was in Laos for a quick stopover. When I told him I was there for the winter to meditate and do yoga, he raised an eyebrow and laughed. "Meditation, huh? I don't get the whole 'calm mind' thing. Does it even help?"

"Hmm," I said, pausing to consider. "I can't say it fixes everything. I still deal with anxiety every day, my thoughts constantly racing. But that's the thing. Meditation isn't about emptying your mind or thinking of nothing—it's about noticing your thoughts. Pay attention tomorrow morning, right after you wake up. I bet your mind will already be racing, making lists, running through a million things before your feet even hit the floor."

He glanced at me, unsure but listening. "So what's the point then?"

"The point is," I continued, "to learn how to let the unimportant thoughts go. To not get carried away by them. It's not about stopping your mind from thinking—it's about recognizing what's worth holding onto, and what you can release."

He seemed skeptical, but I could see a shift in his expression. The wheels were turning. I'd bet anything that the next morning, when he opened his eyes, he noticed his racing thoughts for the first time. Maybe it only lasted a few minutes before his mind whisked him away again, but it's a start. We aren't bodies full of wandering thoughts—we can point our minds where to take us, if we practice enough.

We parted ways at my hotel, exchanging polite goodbyes. I felt the familiar buzz of excitement and nerves as I prepared for three months of spiritual exploration. After unpacking my bag in the hotel room—a simple but warm space with a bed frame made of dark, rich wood that matched the ceiling beams perfectly, creating a canopy-like feel that wrapped the room. The entrance was a set of French doors that opened to the outside, framed by sheer white curtains—it was perfect. I set my alarm for 5 AM and hit the pillow. Tomorrow was the beginning of my quest for enlightenment!

The next morning, my alarm went off, but I hit snooze—typical. After lying there for a few more minutes, I finally dragged myself out of bed thinking, Jesus, enlightenment isn't easy. The early morning light filtered through the thin curtains, and the city was beginning to stir. I had a quiet, mindful breakfast, trying to savor each bite, even though my nerves were building. This wasn't a vacation—I was here to learn something about myself, about the world. After some deep breaths, I stepped out into the streets, my heart pounding with anticipation as I set out to find my first temple.

-ọ-

The temple was beautiful, a serene refuge tucked amidst the quiet streets of the city. The warm red walls were adorned with intricate carvings and golden accents. Towering over everything was a grand golden Buddha, seated in the center of the altar with a gentle, knowing expression. His radiant presence filled the room. The air was thick with the scent of incense, sweet and earthy, curling into the air in thin, delicate spirals. Golden statues of smaller Buddhas lined the walls, each one in a different posture, their faces calm and tranquil. The walls were painted in rich reds and deep maroons, with golden dragons curling up the pillars that supported the temple roof. The roof itself arched high above, its beams painted with vibrant blues and greens, echoing the tropical landscape outside.

I found a corner in the back, feeling small and out of place in such a sacred, vibrant space. A couple of other people were in the temple—a tourist girl sitting at ease in front of the Buddha and an Asian man in quiet meditation. The girl seemed completely at home, her eyes closed in perfect stillness. I wasn't there yet, so I positioned myself near the door, against the farthest wall, trying to blend into the background.

Sitting cross-legged, I set a one-hour timer on my Apple Watch—an insurance policy against quitting early. I began to breathe deeply, counting my breaths as I tried to settle into meditation. The golden Buddha watched over me, his peaceful expression almost mocking the restlessness bubbling inside me. "Breathe in, one; breathe out, two," I counted. My focus shifted between the smooth rhythm of my breathing and the intricate designs etched into the temple's pillars. The red walls seemed to pulse with warmth, their intensity contrasting with the coolness of the hard floor beneath me.

Ten minutes in, I began to feel the creeping discomfort. My back ached, and I kept slouching, glancing up at the radiant Buddha, wondering if my poor posture was some form of disrespect. I couldn't help but notice how bright the fluorescent lights were— unnatural in this ancient, sacred space. If only they had softer, warmer lighting, maybe I could sink deeper into the meditation.

I pulled my hoodie tighter over my head, trying to block out the glaring lights of the temple. The golden statues still glimmered at the edges of my vision, as if they could sense I was faking this whole meditation thing. They knew I was a fraud... I wondered if Buddha was silently judging me from behind that peaceful smile—did he know I was thinking more about my posture and my Apple Watch than any kind of inner peace? I peeked at the time again, willing it to speed up. Five minutes had passed. Only five minutes? Was this supposed to help at all?

I shifted, trying to get comfortable, but my back was killing me. I glanced around, catching the eye of another girl who had walked in. She was moving so slowly, so deliberately, like she was already floating in some zen-like trance. Meanwhile, I couldn't even keep my brain quiet for ten seconds. She glanced at me, probably sensing my total lack of serenity, then quietly slipped back out. Great, now I was being out-meditated by other tourists. I half-expected a monk to come over and drag me out by my hoodie for being a poser. Just another middle-aged white guy trying to fake his way to spiritual enlightenment.

I took another deep breath, determined to make this work. *Inhale, exhale,* I repeated to myself. Maybe if I just kept breathing, I'd stumble into enlightenment by accident. Notice your thoughts, let go of your thoughts. Notice... Oh my god, just yesterday I was a guru, but today, I'm slowly suffocating under my hoodie. I switched tactics.

Okay, mantra time. I racked my brain for something from *Eat, Pray, Love,* because if it worked for Julia Roberts, it should definitely work for me, right? I started mentally repeating the mantra, "the universe is within me as me, the universe is within me as me, the universe is within me as me..." feeling my center coming a bit more to the foreground of my mind. Breathe in, breathe out. But then I immediately got distracted, wondering whether or not I'd ever actually meet the Dalai Lama and whether or not he'd like me. *Focus!* I scolded myself.

I switched again—this time to a visual meditation. I imagined a soft blue light inside me, slowly growing larger. As it expanded, I felt a bit more at ease, so I stretched the light further—enveloping the temple, the Buddha, the tourists outside, and the entire town. When I tried to picture everyone in the town, only the Canadian guy who had shared the cab with me came to mind, so I threw him into my imaginary light bubble, hoping that counted for something.

Feeling more in control now, I kept expanding the light. It swept across Laos, Thailand, China, Sven and his girlfriend, and Laura's family in Hawai'i, Christian in California. The bubble grew even bigger, stretching all the way to France to bless my teachers, my friends, and my family on the other side of the world—Jess, Heidi, Bill, Dan, Mom, Dad. Bless my friends in New York: Mayumi, Laura, Kim, Max, and Ethan's mom. And pop—the bubble was whole. Sweeping across the world in one big mental hug.

An alarm wailed—oh no, my watch! Jolted from my peace and startling the six other people who had quietly joined me, I realized: the hour was up! I had survived—no, succeeded—at my first solo hour of meditation. I made it through the full sixty minutes without running out of the temple screaming. No monks came to judge me, no spies from the heavens, and I only spiraled into a partial existential panic. It felt like a victory.

I peeled the hoodie off my head, taking one last look at the serene Buddha. I stood up, stretched out my sore legs, and slipped back into the early morning routine of the town, relieved—and a little proud of myself for sticking with it.

Back on the street, the fog had thickened, curling through the air like a dream come alive. The usual hum of life was replaced by a reverent stillness, broken only by the soft murmurs of locals arranging food for the procession of young monks collecting their morning alms. Hundreds of boys in vivid saffron robes moved silently through the streets, their bare feet gliding over the cobblestones. I knelt beside a woman who, with quiet kindness, handed me a small pot of rice to offer. In Theravada Buddhism, this daily ritual connects the community to the monks, who walk in silence, copper bowls in hand, to receive their offerings. Each gesture—a scoop of rice, a bowed head—carried profound meaning, an act of generosity and humility earning spiritual merit in return.

As I watched the procession, I couldn't help but think back to my own upbringing. Growing up in Catholic school, the lessons drilled into us were rigid—questions weren't always welcome, and faith often felt like memorizing rules rather than understanding truths. But here, outside this quiet temple tucked into the folds of the Laotian countryside, the air was different. The monks, with their serene smiles and gentle curiosity, seemed to embody something I hadn't seen in my own childhood faith—a calm born not from strict adherence, but from a deeper understanding of the world around them.

The simplicity of the ritual struck me deeply. These monks lived entirely on the kindness of their community, yet they radiated a peace I'd never felt chasing bigger dreams back home. Packing a single bag for this three-month trip, living with almost nothing, had felt daunting at first, but standing there in the quiet haze of morning, it began to feel like a lesson. Material belongings weren't the key to fulfillment. The monks' quiet, unassuming presence seemed to whisper a truth I'd been reluctant to admit: you can let go of the clutter—of possessions, of ambitions, even of fears—and still have enough.

As the procession ended, the mingling scents of morning incense and fried dough lingered in the air, swirling with the first stirrings of the city waking up. It felt as though the world itself was exhaling, and I exhaled with it, letting the quiet settle over me.

Nearby, I spotted a staircase leading up a hill, partially obscured by fog. On a whim, I decided to climb. About halfway up, I passed a man sitting under a tree, he gestured toward a bowl at his side, and I dropped in a few coins before continuing my ascent. The fog thickened as I climbed, wrapping around me like a soft cloak. By the time I reached the top, the world below had disappeared entirely, leaving only the stillness of the moment and the faint sound of my breath.

A golden pagoda greeted me, glowing faintly in the soft light, as if it were generating its own energy. It stood regal and quiet, almost out of place in the foggy world around it. I paused to catch my breath, letting the stillness seep in. The city below was obscured, the outlines of buildings barely visible through the thick mist. There was a quiet beauty in the solitude, as if this hidden part of the world was mine alone to discover.

I caught my racing thoughts, the mental lists piling up as I sped through the day—yoga, errands, tomorrow's plans—but I pulled myself back. *Breathe. Notice your thoughts,* I told myself. *Look out*

over the clouds and be here now, in this moment, not chasing the next one. Experience the now—the mountain in the morning fog. *This is where you are, right now. Be here.*

I turned back down the staircase, feeling a new sense of purpose. But soon, the familiar tick tick tick of my racing thoughts took over, guiding me aimlessly to the next task on my mental list. *Find a yoga or meditation center. Establish a routine for the next few weeks.* The chaos of life back home still had its grip on me, but I could feel myself slowly releasing it.

By 7:00 a.m., I had already found a yoga place across town, offering a class on the riverbank every morning at 7:30. The streets were beginning to wake up as I hurried through the city, shops opening their doors, the clinking of coffee cups, and the low rumble of motorbikes weaving through the narrow streets. I followed the curving alley around Mount Phousi, the fog still lingering in the air like a soft blanket.

Soon, I stumbled upon a small café called Utopia. Its wooden sign boasted, "Chill in the morning, groovy at night." The place had a unique and haunting charm. The cocktail tables were made from old bombs discovered in rice paddies, relics of the US carpet bombing during the Vietnam War. Disarmed and harmless now, these metal shells had been repurposed as furniture, blending the area's painful history with its present-day resilience. It was certainly a place where you felt a need to reflect. Inside, a handful of people gathered near a wide deck that overlooked the Nam Khan River, their faces offering the same kind of wonder and nervous excitement I felt.

This was to be part of my home for the next 14 days, though for most of them, it was just another stop on their endless journey through Southeast Asia. Light lavender yoga mats were laid out across the wooden deck in uneven rows. I chose one close to the front, positioning myself to take in the river. The soft calls of birds echoed through the morning air, their songs mingling with the quiet rustling of leaves. I took a deep breath and closed my eyes, settling into a short meditation before class began.

I could hear the faint trickle of the muddy river as it flowed past, mirroring the steady flow of my breath. Thoughts came and went, judgments floated by, but for once, I didn't chase them. They drifted downriver, like the fog drifting off the water, fading into the distance. I felt lighter.

When I opened my eyes, the teacher had taken their place at the front of the deck. There were no golden Buddhas here, no grand temples or monks to impress me with their presence. It was me, the river, the fog, and the gentle hum of the universe. The class began, and I finally started to find the sense of ease in the practice that I had been searching for. The motions were familiar, but in this place, they felt different. More intentional, more peaceful. I moved through the poses with a quiet confidence, letting the connection between my breath and body guide me.

In the stillness of the morning, on the banks of the Nam Khan River, I felt at peace. And for the first time in a long time, that peace felt real.

An hour later, as I stepped out of the café, the warm air hit me, and I noticed a small cluster of faded, sun-bleached flyers taped to the wall outside the door. Most of them advertised yoga classes, local tours, or traditional cooking lessons. But one stood out—a long, hand-written letter that seemed a bit more personal. It caught my eye immediately. Scrawled across the top were the words: "Help Needed! Native English Speakers Wanted to Teach Kids."

Intrigued, I snapped a quick photo of the flier. It had that earnest, grassroots feel, like someone really needed help. The letter went on to explain how they were looking for volunteers to help local kids practice their English. A part of me lit up at the idea. Maybe this was the kind of experience I had been searching for, something more meaningful than sightseeing.

I typed the email address at the bottom of the flier into my phone and sent off a message without hesitation:

Hi, I'd love to volunteer at your school. I'm here for a few weeks and can come in as much as you need. Best, Luke.

This potential detour became the most exciting part of my trip. I spent the rest of the day checking my phone, hoping for a quick reply, but there was nothing. My mind immediately jumped to doubt—had I mistyped the email? Did it bounce back? Maybe it was an old flier? But then I remembered the Facebook address listed. I pulled up the photo again and searched for their page online. A few taps later, I found it, liked it, and left a message on their wall, eager to make sure they saw my interest.

To my surprise, a messenger bot popped up almost instantly, asking if I wanted to contact them directly. Of course, I did! I sent another message through the bot, throwing out a silent wish that this time it would land where it needed to.

Later that evening, a notification lit up my phone. They had responded! They asked if I could come teach English at a local school on Friday. The idea filled me with both excitement and nervous anticipation. After my usual morning yoga and meditation routine, the plan was set—Sonny, the school's founder, would pick me up at 4 p.m.

As promised, Sonny pulled up right on time. He greeted me with a friendly smile and shared the story of how he had built this school on an empty lot next to his family home, with small makeshift classrooms made of cinder blocks and tin roofs, each with several rows of desks and a whiteboard at the front of the room. His goal was simple but noble: to help local children learn English affordably, giving them more opportunities for their future. As we drove through the town, he spoke with a quiet but steady passion about how important this work was for the community. I was inspired by his dedication.

In the classroom though, my nerves kicked in a little, I didn't really know what I was doing. The first class was with young kids, their wide eyes watching me curiously as I stumbled through my introduction. They didn't understand much English, and I was acutely aware of how out of my element I was. The kids were fidgeting, and I could feel the energy starting to build into restlessness.

Just when I thought I might lose them entirely, Sonny stepped in. His calm, easy manner commanded their attention immediately. One by one, he had each kid write down English words in their notebooks. Then, in turn, they came up to practice the entire vocabulary list with me, repeating each word carefully. "Dog," "table," "car"—simple words, but their enthusiasm was palpable.

And let me tell you, these kids were the epitome of cuteness, their tiny voices saying "helicopter" with so much determination. Most of them did exceptionally well as we worked through the list, except for "calculator"—that word seemed to trip them up every time. But honestly, in that moment, "calculator" was the least of anyone's worries. It was clear these kids were eager to learn, and being a small part of their journey felt like something special.

As I left that day, I couldn't help but smile. I had come here in search of peace, but I was starting to realize that connection—real,

♡

human connection—was the best form of peace I could find.

After about 45 minutes of drilling vocabulary words and sharing laughs, the class wrapped up. Sonny asked us all to gather for a group photo, and soon I was surrounded by the kids, who seemed thrilled that I'd joined them today. It was pure joy—like I'd become a part of something much bigger, even if just for a short time.

As I made my way toward the shop area, Sonny handed me a water bottle, and I noticed a few teenagers rolling in on bikes. They looked like my next class. One girl, smiling wide, approached me and started chatting in English. To my surprise, she was really good.

"Where are you from?" she asked, her voice filled with curiosity.

"New York," I said, watching her eyes light up.

She practically bounced with excitement, going on about how she'd always dreamed of visiting New York, imagining the tall buildings, Times Square, and all the fun it would be. We exchanged Instagram handles like we were already old friends, and she filled me in on her life here before class even began.

This group of teens was more advanced than the little kids. They grasped my introduction quickly as I told them about my photography, the countries I'd visited, and how this was my first time in Laos. The teacher opened the floor for questions. Almost immediately, one of the students in the front row eagerly raised a hand.

"Are you married? Do you have a girlfriend?" the student asked with a playful grin.

Ah, the big question—one that is super awkward in a communist country. I chuckled, shaking my head. "Nope, no girlfriend. I'm traveling solo."

After the obligatory personal questions, the conversation shifted to more meaningful ones: What's life like in New York? What do

I do there? What's my favorite part of traveling? The energy in the room shifted as we got into deeper territory. I pulled out my phone and showed them my website, some of my photography, and even pictures of my house. The students were fascinated, leaning in as I passed the phone around. I shared my Facebook and Instagram details with them, and the idea that they could follow my journey beyond this classroom made them light up even more.

As the questions started to dwindle, the teacher pulled out a worksheet. It was a short paragraph about a teacher doing crafts with her students, followed by a list of vocabulary words. We took turns, with me reading a sentence aloud and the students repeating after me. The quiet kids who were more reserved at the start were responding with so much enthusiasm, their pronunciation impressively accurate.

The more time I spent with the students, the more I came to understand the challenges Laos faces as one of the poorest nations in the world. Communism here isn't as overt or militaristic as it is in China—you might not even realize it's a communist state—but the government quietly controls industries and resources. Yet staggering poverty persists: 90% of the population lives on less than $3 a day. For many families in small farming villages, sending their children to monasteries offers the best chance at a free education—often the highest quality available. In many ways, these monasteries reminded me of how my siblings and I attended Catholic schools in America, just swapping out our pressed uniforms for orange robes. Watching these young monks seek structure, knowledge, and a chance at a better future struck me deeply.

Amidst the hardship of this country, something shifted within me. Helping these students, even in small ways, began to feel like a truer measure of success. It wasn't about climbing a ladder or chasing dreams built on illusions of fame and fortune. It was about being present, sharing knowledge, and finding joy in the simple moments—one word, one sentence, one laugh at a time.

This realization inspired me to take action. I set up a GoFundMe campaign to raise funds for Sunrise English Classroom, the very school where I'd been teaching. I poured every ounce of energy I had into crafting the perfect pitch—writing heartfelt descriptions, selecting captivating photos of the students, and recording a video to convey the urgency of the cause. I wasn't sure if people would respond to the needs of a small school in a remote part of Laos, but I knew I had to try.

To my astonishment, the support came pouring in. Friends, strangers, even distant acquaintances I hadn't spoken to in years—all contributed. By the end of the campaign, I had raised enough money to fund 60 scholarships for local children, providing them with the opportunity to study English, a skill that could open up new horizons for their future. It also helped build a brand-new classroom—more than four walls, it became a space of possibility, a place where dreams could take shape.

The impact was far more profound than I ever imagined. I stood there, camera in hand, capturing the wide-eyed wonder of kids learning their ABCs, watching their faces light up as they grasped new words. Each click of the shutter felt like freezing a moment of pure hope, of lives being subtly but surely changed. Seeing the joy on their faces, the determination in their eyes, and feeling their gratitude—it was unlike anything I'd ever experienced. Every smile, every burst of laughter, every small victory in that classroom left an indelible mark on my heart. The rewards, though not monetary, were far greater than anything I had achieved. For the first time, it felt like

I had found a way to turn my passion for creativity into something that genuinely mattered. Something bigger than me.

During my time in Laos, I had fallen into a rhythm: morning yoga, meditation, teaching English—it all felt like I was finally aligning my life with a deeper sense of purpose. One evening, I decided to attend the evening prayer at a temple, hoping to experience the peaceful chanting of monks. I arrived a bit late, and as I walked into the dimly lit temple, I quickly realized that I had missed the chanting. The stillness in the air felt heavy, almost as if the moment had passed without me.

Not one to give up, I wandered over to a smaller, more intimate temple nearby. The room was warm and inviting, its red walls adorned with mirrored tile accents that caught the evening light streaming through open windows. An altar stood at the far end, a stunning collection of golden Buddhas, each one glimmering with a quiet radiance. One statue, towering overhead, gazed peacefully down at the room, its presence commanding yet serene, as if watching over the monks with gentle wisdom. The rhythmic chants of the monks gathered in a circle flowed through the air like a gentle lullaby.

I sat quietly at the back, the towering Buddha and its smaller companions seeming to watch over me too. I tried to meditate, but the buzz of thoughts in my mind made serenity feel just out of reach. Still, I stayed, the golden gaze of the statues and the hum of the chants grounding me, even if only faintly, as I hoped for some connection.

After the ritual ended, a young monk, Kham Li, approached me with a wide smile. He told me the other monks had been too nervous to talk but wanted to, and he asked if I'd practice English with them. I agreed, curious and excited about what was to come. We sat around a small, humble table—six teenage monks, their robes a striking orange against the temple's earthy tones. I half-expected them to pull out an English textbook, but instead, they simply began asking me questions—about my life, my travels, and, of course, New York City.

As we chatted, Kham shared his story. He'd been living as a monk since he was young, devoted to a life of purpose that made his farmer parents proud—he hoped to lead others in the monastery someday. We bonded over that small porcelain tiled table, sharing stories. When I showed them photos of New York City on my phone, their wide-eyed wonder was palpable. They had never seen anything like it before—the towering skyscrapers, the bustling streets. It was surreal, sharing pieces of my world with them, and in turn, learning about their lives in the monastery.

For the next hour, we exchanged stories, practiced English, and laughed at the differences—and similarities—between our worlds. As I said goodbye, the monks all added me on Facebook, their eagerness to stay connected making me feel like I had just made a group of new friends.

Walking back to my hotel that night, my phone buzzed with messages from them—small, simple "hellos" that brought a smile to my face. It had been a challenging day, but this moment, this connection with Kham Li and the monks, had turned it around. I felt grateful for the experience, for the chance to teach them English and to bond with such thoughtful, kind souls. It reminded me, once again, that no matter how far from home you are, the simplest connections can make the world feel like a much smaller, more welcoming place.

After a long night studying with the monks, I found myself returning to the temple the next day, eager to continue exploring this connection I felt deepening in Laos. It wasn't about learning anymore—it was about something more personal, more profound. The country's tranquil rhythms seemed to be working their way into the cracks of my grief, helping me process the loss of Ethan in ways I hadn't expected.

That morning, the temple felt quieter than usual. As I wandered through the grounds, I met a young monk who was alone, tasked with watching over the temple while the others were at school. He greeted me with a warm smile, and soon, we fell into easy conversation. His presence was calming, a reflection of the peace I had been trying so hard to find.

At some point in our conversation, the monk asked me softly, "Do you ever feel lonely?"

His words struck me. There was a depth in his question, a kind of vulnerability that resonated. He told me about his parents, how they had passed away when he was just a boy. He confessed that not a day went by when he didn't think of them. "Each day," he said, "my heart still hurts."

Hearing his story, I felt a familiar ache rise in my chest. I sat there, deeply empathetic, feeling the weight of his sorrow, and shared my own story. I told him about Ethan, how his passing had left a hole in my life that I was still trying to mend. "He left this world too soon," I admitted, my voice quieter now. "But I carry him with me, even here, halfway around the world. He walks alongside me in everything I do."

The monk listened intently, his eyes filled with understanding. I continued, explaining that his parents, much like Ethan, still lived on in his thoughts, in his joys, and even in his sorrows. "Their love," I said, "travels with you every step of the way. Even though they aren't physically here, they are always with you. Every time you remember them, speak about them, or feel their presence in a quiet moment, you give them life again." I paused, feeling the weight of my own words. "They are all here with us in this temple today—your mom, your dad, Ethan. By sharing their memories, we've brought them into this moment. You've given a piece of them to me, and I will carry them on my journey, too. In that way, they live on."

We sat in silence for a while, the weight of our shared grief settling around us. But it wasn't a heavy, suffocating silence. It felt almost... healing. As if, in that moment, by acknowledging our pain together, we had lightened the burden just a little.

A few days later, I reached out to the monks, asking if I could photograph them in their temple before I left. I wanted to capture their lightness, their laughter, and the lessons I'd come to cherish. The next morning, I woke up late to find a message saying they were free, so I quickly grabbed my camera and hurried over after breakfast.

When I arrived, they were gathered around a small picnic table, practicing their English. Smiles and jokes filled the air as I fumbled with my camera, breaking the ice with a few awkward attempts at small talk. We wandered the temple grounds together, the boys giggling as I tried my best to direct them like some kind of professional photographer.

Eventually, we found our way inside the temple. A golden Buddha statue bathed in soft sunlight from the window became the perfect backdrop. I asked Kham Li, the oldest of the boys and the one I'd connected with the most, to sit for a photo. He understood immediately, his calm demeanor offset by the shy smile he couldn't quite hide. Each of the monks took turns posing, their excitement infectious. The photos turned out better than I'd hoped—each one a mix of reverence and playfulness, a reflection of the joy they carried even in their simple, disciplined lives.

When the session wrapped, the monks quietly headed off to lunch, leaving me to walk back to the guesthouse. My camera felt heavier than usual, filled not just with photos but with a sense of connection I hadn't expected. It wasn't just about capturing images—it was about holding on to the light these boys shared, the sense of calm they seemed to radiate.

Back home, I turned those photos into a book for everyone who had donated to the school. I called it *The Noble Path,* threading my journey through Southeast Asia with the wisdom I'd picked up along the way. Each chapter touched on something I'd learned, weaving together stories of vibrant landscapes, quiet temples, and the lessons the boys had unknowingly gifted me. It wasn't perfect, but it was honest—an attempt to share the gratitude I felt for the moments that had changed me.

Still, the young monk's words lingered: "Do you ever feel lonely?"

I carried that question with me, through oceans and continents, unable to fully answer it. And yet, standing in that temple, surrounded by their quiet giggles and stillness, I began to understand. Loneliness had followed me everywhere, but it wasn't just mine—it was a thread connecting me to everyone who's ever felt its weight. In their light and laughter, I found a kind of peace— not in the way I expected, but in a quiet, unassuming moment that settled over me, offering the faint beginnings of clarity in a complicated world.

I wasn't healed. Not yet. But maybe, for the first time, I believed I could be.

Chapter 10
Mad Men

Back in the fast-paced rhythm of New York, my artistic career finally hit its stride. The city's vibrant, relentless energy was the perfect backdrop for the creative wave I was riding. I became a contributor to Getty Images and Shutterstock, as well as the freelance staff photographer for special events at the Public Theater. Before long, my photographs even popped up in *The New York Times*, capturing moments from the city's most prestigious events. Suddenly, I found myself in the same orbit as celebrities like Anne Hathaway and Tom Hanks—though "rubbing elbows" might be a stretch. I was behind the lens, immortalizing their red-carpet moments.

Around this time, Instagram was taking off. What started as a platform for selfies and sunsets had become a launchpad for artists. I jumped in, sharing photos from Asia, behind-the-scenes shots of my process, and my artistic journey. Little by little, my following grew, and before long, a gallery in the Lower East Side invited me to showcase a solo exhibition of my paintings exploring Eastern religious philosophies. I titled it *Made in Taiwan*—a play on words juxtaposing mass consumerism with spirituality. The collection sought to bridge cultural gaps, capturing the profound beauty of Taoism, Hinduism, and Buddhism on canvas. By portraying gods in a simplified yet ultra-commercial pop art form, I helped American audiences connect with traditions they might never have encountered, reinterpreting their depth and spirituality in a way that resonated across cultures. On opening night, the gallery was packed, and the response was overwhelming. Somewhere between the applause and the congratulations, my art even landed on the cover of a popular gay magazine—a twist I hadn't seen coming. And yet, in her thick Iowa accent, my mom still says, "Oh, Luke, I just wish you'd paint more of those pretty Eiffel Towers!"

Not long after, my work caught the attention of the Art Directors Club Gallery, where a full series of my paintings was picked up for exhibition. Suddenly, my name was floating in conversations I'd only dreamed of, and collaborations started coming my way. One of the most surreal moments came when Dylan's Candy Bar—yes, Ralph Lauren's daughter's candy empire—commissioned me to create a premier collection of pop-art candy paintings. Vibrant, bold, and bursting with energy, they were like a sugar rush captured on canvas. I worked with a buzz of excitement in my studio, knowing this was exactly where I wanted to be.

The collection got plenty of attention, and much to Laura's delight, it even appeared on an episode of a hit Bravo reality TV show. Seeing my work on-screen in such a high-profile way was surreal. It felt like every door I'd ever knocked on was finally swinging open at once.

But New York wasn't done with me yet. My art was showcased at amfAR's (the American Foundation for AIDS Research) high-profile gala, a dazzling event filled with celebrities, activists, and influencers. Seeing my work hanging there was humbling—like a checkpoint on the marathon of my career. And then came one of the most personal and meaningful projects of all: a commission from the Matthew Shepard Foundation. They asked me to paint a portrait of Matthew, a young man whose life was brutally taken in an act of hate that shocked the nation. The devastating violence he endured at the hands of small-town bullies was a haunting reminder of the prejudice I had faced growing up. The portrait was presented to his mother in Washington, D.C., as part of a commemoration of his life. It was the kind of project that stays with you forever.

Recognition kept rolling in. Shortly after, I was stunned to learn GLAAD had named me one of the top 100 artists of the year. GLAAD's acknowledgment felt deeply personal. To be celebrated not just for my art but as part of a movement advocating for equality and identity in the LGBTQ+ community was a kind of validation I hadn't realized I needed.

And yet, the elusive million dollars? Still nowhere in sight. No matter how much I achieved, the money side of things stayed stubbornly the same. The days of Andy Warhol's meteoric rise were long gone, and the fantasy of cashing in like a movie montage just wasn't the reality. If I wanted to get ahead, I had to evolve. So, I dove headfirst into the digital world.

The interactive memorial I'd created for Ethan had been my first taste of what was possible, and as it took off, so did my day jobs in innovation and advertising. Suddenly, I was in the right rooms, pitching to big firms, landing contracts, and finding my footing in a new industry. It was exciting—chaotic, sure—but exciting. Influencer marketing was just starting to take off, and for the first time in my life, I wasn't scraping by. Ten times my Cheesecake

Factory paycheck was coming in, and I even had a real savings account. Credit cards were a thing of the past. Life was timesheets, budgeting, and adulting—but hey, I could make it work.

It wasn't exactly the glamorous Mad Men fantasy I'd imagined, but it wasn't bad either. Boardrooms, cocktail parties, late nights on rooftop bars—it all felt thrilling in a way. My ambition had evolved, and I was finally carving out what my parents would call "legitimate work experience."

Advertising at the time felt electric. Healthcare was shifting from a cold, transactional business-to-business vibe to something personal, something that connected with people. With Obamacare rolling out, we were practically rebranding the whole industry. It was big, bold, and honestly, kind of inspiring.

Amid all the chaos, I pitched an idea I thought was gold. Laura—who'd wowed everyone with her aerialist campaign for the rising health platform Social Workout—was perfect for the next step. Imagine the scene: von Hottie on a nationwide tour, bringing her energy to small towns across America, leading fitness classes, and inspiring people to get active. It was pure middle-America magic— relatable, heartfelt, and undeniably Laura.

We were already planning the tour—calendars, logistics, everything—but, as often happens in advertising, the clients took a different route. They hired a perfectly nice actress, but she didn't have Laura's spark. She wasn't von Hottie. The campaign lost its soul, and the project fizzled.

On paper, I was thriving. Big-name accounts, recognizable campaigns—everything I'd wanted seemed to be lining up. But beneath the Midtown Manhattan gloss, I couldn't shake the feeling that I didn't quite fit. The success I'd chased for so long was within reach, but the allure of it had started to fade.

I found myself grappling with questions I couldn't ignore: Why can't I keep this up? Why does "making it" the traditional way feel so disappointing? I wished my art and photography could just pay the bills. Maybe, after all the adventures I'd had, this office life felt like trying to fit into someone else's story. But there was that voice in the back of my mind urging, *Kid, this is it. Just sit here for a few more years, and the million-dollar dream is yours.* All I had to do was wait it out—like my dad clocking in at the John Deere, only this time the factory came with glass walls and free coffee.

But, like so many of us, each morning, I felt the weight of the day pressing down on me—a cycle of meetings, endless tasks, and eventually just doing what I was told. I was a cog in a machine, going through the motions, waiting for the chance to finally break free. That relentless pull to escape kept tugging at my mind, but this time, it wasn't my dad's foundry hellscape—it was a shiny Midtown office tower.

I was trying to play the game. I kept my head down, did the work, cashed the paychecks. And I was good at it, but with every client brief and endless conference call, I felt like pieces of my spirit were being chipped away. Somehow, painting giant canvases had been traded for suits, late nights at the office, and corporate lunches. But somewhere outside that Midtown grind, the call to create, to dream, and to build something that was truly mine still whispered to me.

I'd sit at my desk, staring out the window, watching the city pulse below and wondering, *What's the point of all this?* I was just selling people on rebranded versions of the same tired Cap'n Crunch schemes—only now, it was pills to cure cancer, erectile dysfunction, or rheumatoid arthritis. I had an honest chance at that million-dollar dream—which was everything I thought I wanted. And yet, something inside me was screaming to break free, to stop following the rules and finally start making my own.

So I started taking on freelance clients at night. It wasn't about the extra cash—it was about reclaiming that creative spark. In a way, it reminded me of what I'd watched my mom do during the tough years when she balanced raising us kids, working at the bakery, and going back to school. She never waited for someone to hand her permission—she made her own path.

She taught us that there's power in creating your own opportunities, even when the odds feel impossible. I'd see her come home from class, exhausted but determined, sitting down with her notes anyway. It wasn't just about earning a degree—it was about taking control of her future. She proved to herself—and to us—that it was possible to break free from the limits of the world we knew.

When I started freelancing, I wasn't just chasing a new dream—I was chasing that same drive I had seen in her. She'd managed work, school, and family, and even earned her master's degree in her 40s. Watching her rewrite the rules taught me it was possible to create a life that didn't fit anyone else's mold. If she could push against all odds, so could I. For the first time, I wasn't just dreaming about a bigger life—I was starting to believe I could create one.

One of my first freelance gigs was with a client in the wedding dress industry. As I dove into the project, that old spark flared up again. This was what I'd been missing—the freedom to explore, to build something new. The project wasn't just about selling dresses; it was about connection. Women across the country were sharing their wedding photos—real women of all shapes, sizes, and stories—filling their feeds with moments that felt raw, honest, and unfiltered. It wasn't airbrushed or overly curated. It was real, and in that authenticity, I saw something powerful.

For the first time in a long time, I felt like I wasn't just working—I was creating something that mattered.

The ideas started flowing, and before I knew it, I was pitching them a concept: let brides-to-be search these real images by dress size, streaming candid moments that catalogs or stores just couldn't capture. It wasn't just about convenience; it was about helping women see themselves in others, making them feel less alone in the search. For the first time, I began to understand that work could be more than meeting deadlines—it could connect people across the globe.

It felt revolutionary—a new connection between the product and the people. The website looked incredible, with Instagram photos streaming across the pages. But logistically, we hit a wall: Instagram didn't have the deeper analytics we needed, and the budget wasn't there to take it to the next level. Still, it lit a fire in me. I knew I couldn't stop there.

So just like that, I launched an app.

By now, you know me—I push, push, and push some more until something happens. That's my M.O. Laura knew this too, though I suspect my unrelenting drive could be a *little* overwhelming at times. But she trusted me enough—or maybe she just had some extra fairy dust lying around—to say yes to becoming my co-founder. What she didn't know? I'd already hired the developer. There was no turning back; we were in motion. Laura was roped in as my partner-in-crime—just like Jess in our childhood schemes—into my biggest idea yet.

At the time, apps were the golden ticket, the next million-dollar idea. Commercials bombarded TV screens with: "There's an app for that!" It was the new frontier for anyone looking to strike it rich. And me? Well, I've never met a marketing pitch I didn't fall

for. But this time, it felt different. I *knew* we had something special.
Laura brought her unique brand of creativity and quirkiness to
the table. Sure, she wasn't an app producer, but Laura could juggle
anything: staplers, galas, awards, and now apps. She was like a human
Swiss Army knife: writer, performer, daughter of a Hawaiian cattle
rancher, and all-around princess enthusiast. Together, we were a pair
of dreamers, ready to disrupt the world with our rainbow-unicorn
fashion app.

We poured ourselves into developing *Cinderly*, the fitting-room
fairy godmother. The concept was simple: users could upload and
tag their dressing-room selfies, creating a visual search engine for
clothing by size. But it wasn't just a tech tool—it was a celebration
of body positivity and authenticity. From the start, we took trolling
seriously, declaring the app a troll-free zone. Users were greeted with
a warning: "The Cinderly kingdom is a troll-free zone. If you troll
here, you will be banished to a kingdom far, far away from far, far
away." To proceed, they had to agree: "I promise not to be a troll."
After all, I'd spent enough of my life dodging jeers; I wasn't about to
allow them in our fairy kingdom.

Laura and I were all in, working full-time to bring this vision
to life. We knew we had something magical—something that could
make people feel fabulous with just a tap of a button. And then,
out of nowhere, the opportunity of a lifetime landed in our laps:
a chance to pitch at a big-time tech conference in front of Silicon
Valley investors. This idea, born from napkin sketches and late-night
brainstorming, was about to take center stage.

Laura and I had to level up—and fast. She suited up in her hot-
pink blazer, her blonde hair styled in a pompadour, looking every
inch the goddess of app development. I, meanwhile, tried to hype
us both up, even as I felt like I was faking it the entire time. We had

one shot to sell this dream, and I couldn't shake the feeling we were way out of our depth. We played it cool, confidently telling the conference folks, "Oh, we've just hired our dev team. This app? It's remarkable."

Our pitch deck sparkled with every ounce of our personalities—rainbows, glitter, and all the whimsy we could muster. It was everything we wanted the app to embody: joy, inclusion, and a little bit of magic. But inside, I was barely holding it together. Every polished line and slick phrase felt like a bluff in a high-stakes game we weren't quite ready for. It was thrilling and overwhelming, like wearing costumes we hadn't quite grown into, praying no one would notice.

And then came the call. The verdict. *"You were unanimously accepted!"* The words hung in the air, almost too surreal to believe. Laura and I locked eyes, wide-eyed, feeling the weight of it settle in. This was it—the chance to take our wildest dreams and turn them into something real, something big.

This wasn't just *any* moment. This was *the* moment. We were going to New Orleans, ready to pitch our dream to the top app investors in the country. The first angel investor of Twitter, Chris Sacca, was speaking at the conference and would be there. Even better, the conference website boasted that the year prior, several companies had walked off the tradeshow floor with three million dollar checks in their hot little hands. For the first time, the million-dollar dream felt close enough to touch. Sure, we had a few setbacks in development—okay, so the app wasn't *technically* finished—but a little thing like that wasn't going to stop us from demoing the heck out of it.

As the days ticked down to the big tech conference, we were caught in a whirlwind of excitement. Sharpening our pitch, tightening our slides, rehearsing like mad—it was startup adrenaline at its finest. Derek, a guy I'd met on a hook-up app and promptly hired as our CFO, suggested we test the pitch on his boyfriend, the CEO of a major champagne brand owned by Beyoncé and Jay-Z. Legit B-E-Y-O-N-C-É!!! I could have died.

When we stepped off the elevator at Roc Nation's offices, it was a *scene*. Lavish doesn't even begin to describe it. Gleaming awards, posters dripping with iconic pop culture moments, and a giant masterpiece of Rihanna's album cover on the wall—it was the fanciest office I'd ever been in. There we were: two scrappy entrepreneurs about to pitch our app in a world far glitzier than anything we'd imagined. I couldn't help gawking and thinking, *Don't screw this up.*

Our warm-up meeting was with the Marketing Director, and she was instantly smitten with us—and the logo I'd designed: a sparkly magic wand, perfectly capturing the imagination of our brand. She leaned in with a mischievous smile and said, "Hey, I've got an idea... Why don't you really lean into this? Dress up in a fairy costume at the conference—with a magic wand in hand. Trust me, that'll get you noticed." It was absurd, but we loved it. Standing out was *our thing.*

Then came the pitch. Of course, I went first—like a lamb to slaughter. Let's just say my delivery didn't quite pop like the bottles they were selling. "So, uh, Cinderly... it's basically your, um, dressing room fairy godmother," I started, trying to gather my thoughts. "We're a data-driven app... matching users with others who are, uh, the exact same dress size on the backend, you know, so they can calculate... like, more accurately... what'll look good on them." Their faces tilted in unison, clearly trying to follow my train of thought.

That's when Laura stepped in, all poise and charm, her voice smooth as silk. "Picture this," she began, her confidence cutting through the room. "Imagine every shopping trip comes with a personal recommendation based on real people who are exactly your size. No more guesswork, no surprises—just confidence." She let the idea hang for a beat, then added, "Our app isn't just data—it's like having a best friend in the fitting room. A fitting-room Fairy Godmother! And the star ratings? It's a gut-check, like your most honest friend saying, 'Yes, girl,' or 'Maybe try another.'"

There were a few nods around the table now. Laura leaned in just enough to seal the deal. "We're bringing back that magic moment of trying on clothes but making it accessible from anywhere, anytime. With a touch of fairy dust, but no champagne required... though we wouldn't say no." She winked.

The CEO cracked a smile, and I knew we had them. Laura had absolutely knocked it out of the park, leaving the kind of impression that makes you feel like you could pitch a million-dollar idea to anyone. And as the glow of our champagne-popping pitch settled in, an opportunity of a lifetime landed in my lap: a casting call for Apple's new reality show, *Planet of the Apps*. Think *Shark Tank* for app makers—how could we not go for it?

We threw ourselves into it, creating a YouTube series called *Founder Friday* to break down the craziness of building an app— with plenty of sparkles and laughs. The producers couldn't get enough of our quirky charm and wild ideas. We made it through multiple rounds, and fame felt just a few pitches away. But, in classic startup fashion, there was a plot twist: our developer was based in Australia, and that tiny detail knocked us out in the final round. Our Hollywood moment? Poof—like glitter in the wind.

Still, our brush with reality TV wasn't over. Laura's college buddy, Mitchell—now a TV producer—caught wind of our potential rise to stardom and jumped on board. He rushed to film us pitching our sparkling app. Since my loft was off Wall Street, we came up with a wild idea: take it to the streets and shake down some big financial investors for money! There we were, crisscrossing the sidewalks of the Financial District—me, styled in my best Mickey Mouse T-shirt, and Laura shimmering as the Blue Fairy, complete with iridescent wings I'd bought specifically for the conference. We suited up and set out to pitch investors right on the streets of New York's financial hub.

So there we were—Laura in fairy wings and a blue dress, cameras rolling as we marched down Wall Street at the height of lunch hour. I approached businesswomen mid-salad, pitching the app like their kale needed dressing-room recommendations. Did they look like our future investors? Maybe. Did they *act* like it? Absolutely not. Despite their killer outfits, none of them wanted to buy into the magic we were selling. But we weren't discouraged. We cornered anyone in a suit who seemed to have a wallet. At one point, Laura even asked a guy out after pitching him the app. Multitasking! He declined both offers, though I'm pretty sure he was more into me.

Back at my loft—Cinderly HQ—we regrouped with our version of glam. We threw the most ridiculous fashion show you've ever seen for Mitchell's cameras. Laura raided her closet, strutting down our makeshift runway in every sparkling dress she owned, culminating in a full-blown Care Bear onesie, topped off with a CGI Care Bear Stare. (That's right. CGI!)

The video? A smash hit. We were pitched to MTV, Bravo, Logo—all the networks that had me convinced I was about to be a reality TV sensation. It felt like the wedding of Luke and Laura on

General Hospital—over 81 million viewers! Obviously, we were going to top that, right? Wrong. Apparently, no one wanted a long-term series about two scrappy app builders—*shocking,* I know.

Even though none of those pitches turned into cash or fame, we were totally riding the high. After Laura's killer pitch to the CFO, they even gifted us a gold bottle of Ace of Spades champagne. That's when I knew: we could totally do this. Bring on the conference!

The day of our flight was pure chaos. We'd scored last-minute investment cash from my sister Heidi and a few friends, but the night before, I misplaced the check. During the frantic scramble to find it, a massive glass ornament fell off the shelf and smacked me square in the head. The result? A mild concussion. But we weren't stopping now—we grabbed our bags and rushed to JFK, bandaged and determined.

In New Orleans, our big plans to hit a networking pub crawl fell apart in true Cinderly fashion. We rolled up two hours late, thanks to a last-minute crisis involving our sparkling tote bags. (Yes, we splurged on totes.) We'd stashed them in a friend's trailer park north of the French Quarter, cramming them into every corner, assembling them with shaking hands and rising stress. The idea? Flood the conference with dazzling totes and leave a glitter trail behind us. The reality? Sweat, chaos, and a trailer park overflowing with exploding tote bags stuffed with custom sunglasses, buttons, and Cinderly swag. It was like Gucci met Claire's in a glitter-filled showdown.

At the pub crawl, tech people swarmed us with questions. Half the time, they threw out fancy terms I barely understood, but I nodded along like a pro. *Fake it till you make it,* right? Deep down, though, I couldn't stop thinking about the investor meetings. This was it—our big shot.

Luckily, we were staying in style. Derek had hooked us up with a swanky hotel room—a gift courtesy of his very successful boyfriend.

The digs came with free breakfast, which, in the grand scheme of things, felt like striking gold because, let's be real, between the tech talks and tote bags, rest wasn't exactly on the schedule.

In that fancy hotel room, Laura was up early, curling her hair and transforming into the Blue Fairy while the jitters set in for both of us. She shot a frantic text to her friend in Spain, Zelda. *I'm freaking out,* she wrote. *It's gonna be ten thousand bro-dudes in startup tees grilling me on tech stuff I don't know, and I'll have to tell them, "Hello, I don't think you get it, but I'm the new Instagram."* Classic meltdown material.

Zelda's response was spot-on: *What are you wearing?* Laura sent a pic of her shimmering powder-blue dress and fairy wings. Without missing a beat, Zelda posted on Facebook: *Good luck to my girl Laura, the new Fairy Boss Mother!*

And just like that, it clicked. Laura wasn't just playing dress-up—she *was* the Fairy Boss Mother. That title held all the confidence and magic we needed to own the day.

Armed with her new identity, we marched into the conference, wings practically glowing. Our booth? Prime real estate, front and center, baby! Cinderly and the Fairy Boss Mother were ready to dazzle.

But waiting for people to come to us wasn't the vibe. Laura threw caution to the wind, sparkling in her fairy getup, walking right up to attendees with, "Hi! Have you heard of my new app? It's right over here at our booth!" Her energy was magnetic. People started snapping photos, asking, "Who is she?" and I proudly chimed in, "She's the Fairy Boss Mother!" Watching her work the room, I couldn't help but think of my little sister Jess and me, knocking on doors for Cap'n Crunch—only this time, we had fairy dust fueling our scheme. Just like back then, I believed we could take on anything. Laura even caught the twinkling eye of a Saudi investor!

Laura made it her mission to hunt down every press badge in the room, marching up to reporters with, "I bet you want to interview me." And you know what? It worked. We landed interviews with two news channels, a blog, and even a video feature. Watching Laura shine was like watching a star born in real time. Each time someone asked her about being a woman founder, she spoke with the confidence of someone who'd been doing this forever, even though we'd been in the game for all of five minutes.

The truth is, before Laura became the Fairy Boss Mother, we'd been trying way too hard to fit into the serious tech-founder mold—parroting jargon and trying to blend in with the bro-dudes. But that wasn't us. She was a fairy in a sea of T-shirts, and the moment we embraced who we really were, we had more power than any pitch deck could ever offer.

On the second day of the conference, things got... messy. I was stumbling around in a stress-fueled fog (thanks to that probably-more-serious-than-we-thought concussion). Laura had to practically force-feed me granola bars because I hadn't eaten in two days. But we pushed on, bracing ourselves for the investor meetings we'd been building up in our minds as the make-or-break moments. We'd been imagining pitching to men in suits in glossy conference rooms, dazzling them with my sleek video deck, cap tables and business plans bursting from Laura's hot pink folder to tap dance across the table.

Reality, however, had a sense of humor. The investor area was a patch of astroturf in the middle of the noisy conference floor, looking more like a fake grass pet relief station at an airport than the high-stakes meeting space we'd imagined. The vibe? Chaos. Dozens of hopeful entrepreneurs buzzing around, their pitches creating a relentless hum.

When our turn finally came, we sat down, well-rehearsed and brimming with optimism. But the investor had no clue who we were.

Turns out they'd only been handed the startup list that morning. So much for tailored connections.

Undeterred, we launched into our pitch, delivering with all the fairy-tale sparkle we could muster. But the first investor didn't care about apps. The next didn't touch early-stage startups. The one after that? Fin-tech specialists. Why were we even talking to Fin-tech specialists about a fashion app?

There was no million-dollar check waiting for us at the end of the day. Not even a handshake. The investor meetings were a harsh reality check—the conference was more of a trade show filled with other startups trying to pitch *us*. Kind of like the summer I found out Cap'n Crunch was more of a ruse than a jackpot. It was disillusioning, sure, but those fairy wings? They had a way of making us feel invincible, even when reality kept throwing concrete floors at us.

Out of nowhere, a man stepped through the crowd, exuding mystery and confidence. "I'm Turki," he said, handing me a business card that screamed wealth. His assistant, a statuesque woman with long, dark hair, slipped me another card. *This is it,* I thought. *This is how the big deals get done.*

Laura had caught Turki's eye the day before, her fairy wings sparkling across the conference floor. He was an investor from Saudi Arabia, looking for startups that stood out. Big Oil money—I could almost hear the Hollywood soundtrack playing. He invited us to a meeting the next evening at a five-star hotel, and my heart raced. *Finally, our Cinderella moment.*

The next night, we stepped into a lobby that looked straight out of a Bond movie. Chandeliers, plush booths, velvet curtains, and dim lighting that made everyone look expensive. Ushered into a private booth, we met Turki, who greeted us warmly. He wasn't the type to pitch—he let you do the talking first. Laura, with her signature charm, led the way, pitching our app with the confidence of someone who'd been in the game forever. I chimed in with our business plan, casually mentioning our worldwide launch just weeks away. Turki nodded, his eyes glinting with interest.

Then he dropped it: "If you make it to the next round, we'll have another meeting." *Another round?* My mind flashed to *Shark Tank*. It was like playing a private version of the show, velvet booths instead of TV cameras.

After the meeting, Turki leaned back with a grin and asked for a group photo. "I like to keep pictures of my first meetings with potential investments," he explained, his casual air only adding to the mystique. It felt like a scene straight out of *Dynasty*—oil money and all—where opulence clashed with ruthless ambition. Laura and I exchanged quick, nervous glances before putting on our best million-dollar smiles.

We posed in front of the plush velvet booth, trying to exude the kind of effortless confidence you'd expect from startup founders on the brink of success. I was sure the camera caught a flicker of desperation behind my grin, but the way Turki beamed as he snapped the photo gave me a flicker of hope.

As we walked out of the grand lobby, Laura turned to me and whispered, "That photo thing—it's like he's collecting startups like baseball cards, right?" Her voice was light, but her words stuck with me. Was this just another trophy moment for him, or were we genuinely on his radar?

I laughed, more out of relief than anything else. "Well, if we're in his deck, I'm calling us the rookie card," I joked. But deep down, that spark of hope wouldn't die. We'd been invited into the room, into the very spaces where big deals happen. That had to mean something.

Despite our polished pitches, DIY financial charts, and meticulously crafted business plans, we didn't make it to the next round. There was no million-dollar check, no crude-oil-drenched handshake sealing a glamorous deal in that opulent hotel. But strangely, it didn't matter as much as I thought it would.

We had done something extraordinary—we had walked into that room, wings and all, and made people take notice. And for two scrappy dreamers fueled by fairy dust and determination, that felt like a win worth celebrating.

As if the universe was winking back at us, we were named one of the top five startups to watch at the conference. It wasn't the win we imagined, but it was validation. Proof that we belonged in this chaotic, glittering world of tech titans and unicorn dreams. Standing shoulder to shoulder with Laura, I felt it: belief. Belief that we didn't need anyone's permission to make this happen.

Disappointed but determined, we retreated to Miami to regroup. That night, as fate would have it, Chris Sacca—the investor we'd hoped to meet—was appearing on *Shark Tank.* Drinks in hand, we gathered around the TV, ready for some much-needed inspiration.

And then, the unexpected: a fashion app pitched by a competitor took the stage. My heart raced as we watched their presentation, thinking, *This could've been us.* But Chris wasn't impressed. He cut them down, pointing out everything the app was missing. "Not the right fit," he said, with a shrug that crushed their dreams.

It was like a lightning bolt. I grabbed my phone, adrenaline pumping. If Chris didn't like their app, he needed to see ours. Without hesitation, I fired off a tweet: *Chris, you're right, but I've got one for you that sparkles!* I attached a link to our pitch deck, along with the article naming us one of the top five startups from the conference. With a deep breath—and maybe a little liquid courage—I hit send.

And then it happened. Chris Sacca liked our tweet! I nearly exploded with excitement. Without thinking, I jumped up and ran around the hotel pool, shouting, "Chris Sacca liked my tweet! Chris Sacca liked my tweet!" It was pure, unfiltered joy—one of those moments where you feel like you're *this close* to the breakthrough. It felt like the Silicon Valley gods had noticed us and sent down their golden blessing.

Chris didn't come knocking with a checkbook, but that tiny heart-shaped bit of validation was enough to fuel our fire. If one of the biggest names in tech liked us, we knew we had something special. And in true Luke fashion, I figured we needed to capitalize on that moment—so I scraped together $3,000 and bought Justin Bieber tickets.

Yes, Justin Bieber. We gave away a pair to promote the app and ended up at Madison Square Garden ourselves. I even set up a Snapchat filter geo-fenced to the stadium that night. Our tagline? *"This $#!T is B-A-N-A-N-A-S!"* Sparkly logos, confetti, and dancing bananas lit up the screens of thousands of Beliebers. There I was, belting out *Sorry* with a stadium full of fans while our filter racked up hundreds of thousands of shares. From that moment on, I was officially known as Cinderly's *Chief Executive Belieber.* Ridiculous? Absolutely. But it worked. We took the filter on the road, targeting stadiums as Bieber's tour swept across America.

But despite the buzz, the bank account told a different story. Desperate to keep Cinderly alive, I turned to Airbnb. I transformed my live/work artist loft into a rental, and suddenly, people were paying top dollar to stay in a space that felt like Tom Hanks' loft from *Big*. Toys, games, quirky charm—it was a hit. Ironically, another tech platform was now funding our startup dreams.

From a friend's country house in Pennsylvania, I managed it all—sending sketch files to our Australian developer, strategizing with Laura in New York, and running the Airbnb hustle on the side. It was one of those "at all costs" moments, and I wasn't about to let the dream die.

Looking back, it was clear that every hustle—from paper routes to Broadway—had prepared me for this. I'd been steeped in marketing schemes since hunting for Cap'n Crunch sweepstakes as a kid. Those early lessons taught me that success didn't come from waiting—it came from chasing. Every paper delivered, every door knocked on, every scheme dreamed up—it all added up to this. Hustling for Cinderly felt like second nature. Laura and I were scrappy, resourceful, and determined, just like I'd been back on those early paper routes.

The launch of Cinderly felt like a fairy tale come to life. Our magical algorithm matched users with their perfect styles and sizes. We landed meetings with Nordstrom, hired a "growth hacker" for PR, and watched thousands of users sign up in the first week. Fashion influencers flooded the app, creating a spectrum of vibrant styles. For a fleeting moment, it felt like we'd struck startup gold.

But just as quickly, the dream began to unravel. User engagement dropped, influencers moved on, and the platform—once alive with creativity—fell silent. It was like a digital ghost town. Notifications stopped buzzing. The pulse that had powered Cinderly had faded.

I realized then that success could vanish in an instant, no matter how hard you worked or how bright the spark. It was a hard lesson, but maybe one of the most important. The hustle, the creativity, the resilience—it's hard to sustain when things feel impossible. Like a boy with his guitar, I found myself, for maybe the first time ever, truly feeling like hanging it up.

It was as though we had built a thriving metropolis, only to watch it empty overnight. Meanwhile, the colossal presence of Instagram, a social media giant no startup could hope to compete with, loomed larger than ever. We were out of our depth, fighting a battle that felt impossible to win. The only viable option for survival was to pivot—to fully integrate with Instagram and hope that by riding its coattails, we could regain the momentum we had lost. But that shift wasn't just a technical adjustment; it was a complete overhaul, one that required capital we simply didn't have.

The startup game was starting to feel as high-stakes as McDonald's Monopoly. Was it rigged against dreamers like me from the beginning? Not exactly—or at least not entirely. I knew the stakes going in. I had rolled the dice with a dollar and a dream, facing off against billion-dollar business models. We had the brand, a golden idea, and we were so close to making it all the way around the board. Then a chance card came up: *"Pay 10x in utilities."* And just like that, our little engine that could... couldn't make it past *Go.*

The money problem became insurmountable. Without investors to fund development, marketing, and PR, we were sinking fast. I had already emptied nearly my entire savings account, and the hemorrhaging didn't stop there. Hosting thousands of high-resolution photos on servers around the world while running aggressive social media campaigns drained us dry. Each day felt like standing on the deck of a sinking ship, desperately bailing water as the tide rose faster than we could manage. To stay afloat, we needed hundreds of thousands of dollars—an increasingly impossible goal.

It became clear we were on borrowed time. After months of

clawing our way through development, sleepless nights, and endless research, we faced the truth: our dream—the app we had poured everything into—had only six weeks left. The idea of shutting it down after so much hope and promise was devastating. Watching something so full of life wither away felt like losing a piece of ourselves.

In the end, launching (and closing) Cinderly was the kind of experience no grad school or startup incubator could teach. It was a crash course in resilience, ambition, knowing when to pivot—and, ultimately, knowing when to let go.

Believing it would be the magic that reshaped the fashion world, then watching it crumble, was heartbreaking. Picking up the broken pieces of something we had imagined so vividly left us shaken. Yet, as we sifted through the wreckage, something unexpected emerged. From the ashes of Cinderly, I found a new sense of purpose and honed skills I hadn't anticipated.

It wasn't just about coding apps, though I became a better coder than I ever thought possible, tackling development challenges that once seemed insurmountable. Nor was it solely about entrepreneurship, though I sharpened my instincts for pitching, marketing, and crisis management. The failure of Cinderly opened doors I hadn't seen—like launching five quirky, playful games on the App Store. Mermaid Stickers, Poo Stickers, Pretty Pretty Princess games—these whimsical creations turned loss into light, spreading a bit of magic in their own way and racking up nearly 100,000 downloads. All the emojis I'd created for in-app purchases were living their best twinkling afterlife in the App Store.

Cinderly may not have become the fashion app we envisioned, but it became the launchpad for something bigger—a springboard for new ideas and a playground for creativity in ways I hadn't expected. The lesson? Dreams don't always look the way you imagine, but sometimes, the best outcomes come from the most surprising places.

We chased a dream, fought for it, and even when it slipped through our fingers, we walked away with an arsenal of experience and unexpected small successes. Cinderly may have folded, but the journey didn't end there. It was the beginning of a kaleidoscope of personal growth and creative achievements that continue to shape my path forward. In the end, failure wasn't a full stop—it was the break before the next chapter.

Chapter 11
How to $#!T Glitter

As Cinderly's final curtain fell, it felt like a gut punch. The dream I had nurtured, built, and fought for had come crashing down in a sparkling heap. We had poured every ounce of creativity and ambition into that app, and when it didn't work, the disappointment hit hard. The silence after the hustle was deafening, and for a while, I felt lost, unsure of my next move.

But if there's one thing about me, it's that I don't stay down for long. Amid that failure, something unexpected happened—another idea began to shimmer beneath the rubble of Cinderly. It was small, silly even, but it was fun, and after everything, that's what I needed. And if I knew how to do anything after all these years, it was how to turn failure into something that sparkled. Or, better yet, how to $#!T glitter.

That's when Glitter Poo Pills were born, almost by accident—a creation so absurdly unique that it was impossible to ignore. Orders for our tongue-in-cheek pills, filled with shimmering iridescent glitter, poured in like a sparkling waterfall. Clients had the chance to "Poop like a princess" with our "Pretty Pretty Princess Pack" or embrace their inner sea goddess with our "Mystic Seawitch" glitter poo pills. Don't worry, they're safe—my dog would gobble them up off the floor as soon as they fell... which is also how I know they work! In an odd twist of serendipity, what started as a quirky side project became an internet sensation, capturing imaginations across the digital landscape.

At the heart of this preposterous phenomenon was one of our taglines from that fateful conference: "This shit is bananas!" We had joked about it in the early days, but those words took on a life of their own, propelling us to an odd kind of accomplishment I never saw coming. It was a clear sign that even the most unconventional ideas can pave the way for something extraordinary. Glitter Poo Pills were evidence that, despite setbacks, the weird and unexpected can lead to shining little wins—or in this case, a very glittery one.

We sold thousands of dollars' worth of stock, despite the warning on the order form that said in plain English, "DO NOT EAT GLITTER PILLS! If you're determined to turn your insides into a disco ball, that's on you. By swallowing these, you assume full liability for any sparkle-related intestinal adventures—and trust us, your doctors and our lawyers will not be impressed."

So there I was, night after night, sitting at my kitchen table, carefully filling tiny gelatin capsules with glitter I'd bought in bulk from Amazon. Each one glimmered like a little promise of something ridiculous and magical. I slapped a beautiful, hand-designed sticker onto hundreds of plastic bags, sealing them up with a mix of pride and disbelief. Day after day, I packed them, shipped them, and watched as orders kept pouring in—tangible proof that sometimes the most unexpected ideas can catch fire.

Following the glitter-fueled triumph, our momentum skyrocketed on YouTube, where our "Founder Friday" videos captured the hearts of thousands. We even struck gold with a live wedding proposal at a Katy Perry concert—a moment so sweet it practically broke the internet. It was a meteoric rise, and in no time, we hit monetization. We dreamed of creating a pop culture series, expanding our digital empire one quirky video at a time.

But as quickly as we found our small viral success, the rug was pulled out from under us. A massive influencer scandal rocked the YouTube world, and the platform swiftly changed its rules for monetization. These reckless actions not only dominated headlines but shattered the delicate ecosystem for creators like us. In an instant, the Founder Friday video success we'd built was under threat. It felt cruel—the way one person's poor decisions could destroy so much opportunity for others. The system we had worked so hard to break into was now closing its doors, leaving us to pick up the pieces of yet another dream deferred.

But if there's one thing I've learned, it's that even in the most frustrating moments, there's room to pivot. What seemed like the end was just another chapter. I knew we'd find another way—because, at this point, that's what I did best.

And so, with a click of my ruby red Converse heels and a wave of Laura's magic wand, I returned to the beginning. After all, I learned once: there's no place like home; there's no place like home; there's no place like home.

Growing up in those cornfields, on the banks of the mighty Mississippi River, the tradition of baking sweets ran deep in our family. Every weekend, if we weren't scheming and dreaming, my sister Jess and I could be found tucked away in my mom's cherry-colored kitchen, rolling out cookies on her glittery quartz countertop. The flecks of sparkles twinkled like tiny stars under the warm kitchen light, adding a touch of magic to every batch we made. We carefully followed the faded recipe cards from my grandmother's well-worn recipe box, their edges soft and smudged from years of use, trying to recreate the treats that felt like family traditions in every bite. The aroma of sugar and vanilla would fill the air as we perfected every cookie, cake, and pie like they were pieces of art. That countertop was more than a place for baking—it was where Jess, Heidi, Jill, my mom, dad, and brothers all felt at home, connected by the love and warmth that filled the kitchen. So, inspired by my mom and grandma, I flew home to carefully copy their beloved, handwritten recipes onto my MacBook, each one carrying the memory of generations. And with a fistful of fairy dust, I had returned to my roots.

Baking became more than a pastime; it was a source of comfort, a thread connecting me to home, my childhood, and later, to Ethan. I told him once how as a kid I daydreamed about my Lisa Frank, technicolor future, imagining a place where desserts sparkled as brightly as the dreams behind them—my very own Rainbow Cake Café. As a tribute to Ethan, I pulled out the same worn, beaten hand mixer we'd once shared while making soufflés together. With every whirl of its tired blades, it stirred up not just batter, but the memories of laughter, flour-covered counters, and the joy we found in creating something sweet together. He may not have been able to help me out this time, but he was there every step of the way, his spirit guiding me as if he were right beside me. The cookbook became more than just a dream—it was about honoring the sweetness of life and the people who had made it so rich. It was my own personal pièce de résistance.

It was time to bake magic again, this time with a splash of Rainbow Brite inspired whimsy. We transformed my downtown loft into a Pinterest spectacular—a candy-coated wonderland— and launched the Easy Bake Unicorn Cookbook. With a flurry of excitement and a truckload of sugar, Laura and I turned my home into a confectionery circus. From the stove to the makeshift photo studio in the living room, the place looked like Willy Wonka's factory had exploded—rainbow sprinkles, cotton candy, and Funfetti galore.

For weeks, we immersed ourselves in the mayhem of trial and error, perfecting every sticky, vibrant treat we could imagine. I combined my grandmother's classic recipes with a bucket full of food coloring to create masterpieces that would have any unicorn's jaw drop. There were cakes that shimmered like glass slippers, cookies that twinkled, and gooey marshmallow creations that looked straight out of a fairy tale.

In the middle of the chaos, I'd call my mom, the original queen of confections, desperately asking for clarity on the recipes. "Why doesn't my frosting taste like yours?" I'd ask, exasperated as I stared at a bowl of icing that just wasn't right. She always had an answer, a tip to bring the magic back. "Add a little vanilla," she'd say, and "Throw in some edible glitter—go big or go home!" Her advice always felt like a sprinkle of the sparkle she'd infused into my childhood, reminding me that even the smallest touches could make something extraordinary. After all, it wasn't just about baking—it was about carrying forward her flair for turning the ordinary into something magical, just like she did in the bakery at Econofoods, where every cinnamon roll or birthday cake seemed to sparkle with a little extra love.

The whole project was a sugar-fueled bonanza of creativity, with every inch of the loft coated in flour, sugar, and food coloring. My wooden floors were sticky with syrupy concoctions and scattered candy wrappers. Every corner felt alive with the energy of our baking experiments, our ideas growing bolder by the day.

Laura, who'd never been much of a baker, found herself front and center, crushing Oreos for our Dirt Worm Pie and whipping up

Unicorn Hot Chocolate with marshmallows floating like tiny clouds. We filled the days with laughter as she fumbled her way through learning, and Laura and I scrambled to capture each glorious creation in photos for the book. My downtown loft became a sugary dreamland where rainbows truly felt at home.

And so, with every batch of crystalized popcorn balls and every star-dusted cake pop, Cinderly's Easy Bake Unicorn Cookbook came to life. It was a fantastical journey through beloved childhood classics like "Rainbow Cake Nirvana," "Jurassic Park Sugar Cookies," "Peeps Pizza," and more. With vibrant, full-color photography and whimsical touches, we brought baking into the realm of imagination.

The Kickstarter campaign was a wild achievement, surpassing all our expectations. In only seven days, we hit our funding goal, turning what had once been a whimsical idea into a full-blown reality. Support poured in from all corners of the globe—moms, tweens, kids, and bakers-at-heart eager to bring a little extra magic into their kitchens. The excitement was contagious, and it felt like the whole world wanted a taste of the sweet, dazzling fun we were stirring up.

Once the books were printed, they flew off the shelves, finding homes in thousands of kitchens through Amazon and other platforms. It wasn't just a cookbook anymore—it became a movement of creativity, color, and joy. Kitchens that had once been quiet were alive with the sound of laughter, the smell of sugary treats, and the sight of sprinkles and disco dust strewn across countertops. In kitchens from Iowa to Indonesia, the Easy Bake Unicorn Cookbook (unicorncookbook.com) became more than a book—it became a celebration of imagination, one sweet slice of happiness at a time.

Moms told us they used the recipes for birthday parties, family gatherings, and sleepovers. Tweens posted their creations all over social media, tagging us in their rainbow-tinted, sugar-coated masterpieces. Kids, with frosting smeared on their faces, proudly showed off their Unicorn Hot Chocolates and Poo Party Cupcakes as if they'd baked them straight from a magical world. We were named the top children's cookbook by mommy bloggers across the nation.

Looking around at my loft, the floor now dusted in flour and bits of glitz, I realized I had done it. I had returned to the same whimsical, wide-eyed energy that I'd always carried as a kid scheming up big dreams in Iowa, mixing that sense of wonder with a new wave of adventure. What had begun with a few glitter poo pills had exploded into something beautiful—a journey that brought joy to kitchens everywhere, one magical treat at a time.

And so, with a burst of excitement, I turned to Laura and exclaimed, "Let's do it again!" At the time, Laura had been teaching creativity workshops designed to help people overcome their inner critics and embark on their own personal hero's journey. She'd even branded the series "Don't Quit Your Daydream," complete with a journal full of daily prompts and a sparkling rainbow cover that captured the spirit of playful ambition. I'd helped her bring the project to life, never realizing at the time how much her classes would inspire me to take on my own challenge.

Laura's workshops planted a seed. Our own lives had been a hero's journey—full of twists, triumphs, and trolls that deserved to be shared. And once the idea of this book took root, there was no stopping it. I convinced Laura to sit down with me for two whirlwind days, ten hours at a time, where we'd interview each other about our lives, recounting the battles we fought, the challenges we faced, and the moments that made us laugh until we cried.

What you've just read is the product of those interviews— candid, often hilarious, and deeply personal conversations captured on camera. I'll be the first to admit: I'm a decent storyteller. These words were crafted, re-crafted, and shared with my writing group at the Middle Collegiate Church in New York. Heck, I even spent three months in the Philippines cranking out 85,000 words for an entirely different novel. Laura? Sure, she went to school for creative writing and had experience. But turning these wild conversations into a cohesive story wasn't easy. Originally, this book was told from both our perspectives—with me narrating from childhood on and her telling it from Cinderly backward. She taught me lessons along the way. But it was confusing—two writing styles, one voice, arguments, tears, a pandemic, etc.

I knew I had a knack for storytelling and knew the story I wanted to tell. But the actual writing process? That was a whole different beast. I could derive an arc, but I couldn't even spell the word "agian" correctly. I spell "i" before "a" every time—wrong, over and over, forever. Because of my dyslexia, I still cannot physically see it. Yes, autocorrect has helped me immensely, and even my oldest sister Heidi says I'm a remediated dyslexic, meaning my brain has, through years of struggle, found ways to correct mistakes. Heidi even started a dyslexia school in Iowa after witnessing my lifelong battle; she was the first to recognize the signs and suggested I might have the condition. But it's still difficult, especially for this book. I worked on it for years, hired a transcriber, dumped all the content into a Google Doc, and set off on a literary adventure that was as challenging as it was exciting. Laura looked it over, I had a developmental editor, beta readers, people helping with the arc, offering advice...

What unfolded in these pages is based on truth—but it's not the whole truth. It's how I remember it, a blend of reality and the way my mind interprets the past. Writing this book was a monumental challenge, but for the most part, this sparkly tale of friendship, ambition, and adventure had sat on the shelf, gathering dust—until now.

After Laura and I weathered the chaos of surviving Manhattan through COVID, I found myself riding the dizzying highs and crushing lows of the NFT craze—making and losing out on a quarter of a million dollars in what felt like the blink of an eye. Naturally, I also dove headfirst into the "Wall Street Bets" frenzy: I bought DogeCoin at $0.03 and sold it at $0.027, probably making me one of the few to actually lose money on that scheme. But I was too nervous to risk a thousand dollars while unemployed, living on government handouts in a $5,000-a-month loft in Lower Manhattan after my Airbnb scheme dried up. With the future of the city uncertain, I wasn't sure if Manhattan would ever reopen or if I'd even find a job in the post-pandemic landscape. DogeCoin eventually shot up to the moon hitting nearly $1, and I watched another potential $100,000 slip through my fingers. By all accounts, I should have been rich six times over during the pandemic.

But as I thought that chapter of my life was over, I stumbled upon something else—something potentially even more disruptive and dangerous: AI. At first, it appeared to be just another tool, another tech curiosity. I couldn't have predicted how deeply it would shape the next part of my journey.

The truth is, for years, I had collected stories, ideas, and fragments of memories—each one meant to become part of a larger whole. Every time I tried to pull them together, though, my dyslexia threw up walls I couldn't break through. Hubris had always been my great ally, but when it came to writing, I couldn't quite master the technical skills. Spelling, grammar, and even autocorrect barely worked for my mess of a brain. It was like having a million-dollar idea but not knowing how to cash the check.

But I had the words, tons of words, notebooks filled with finished stories, random musings, jokes, and hours of recorded conversations with Laura sat in piles. We'd poured ourselves into those talks, dreaming up adventures, reflecting on our past schemes, and planning for the future. But turning all that chaos into a cohesive narrative—a book people might actually want to read—felt impossible. I didn't have the skills to do it alone, and I didn't know where to start.

And then, there it was—ChatGPT—waiting in the wings like a new partner-in-crime, ready to join me on my next heist. My secret hustler, the one I teased you about on the very first page of this book. But don't get me wrong, this story isn't some love affair. At first, I was skeptical—could a piece of technology really help me tell my story? I gave it a shot, trying to write fiction. I had piles of notes, bits of stories I'd been working on—like one about pirates from my adventures in Thailand or another about how the first Lost Boy in Neverland came to be. But let me tell you, it was horrible. Awful. Completely terrible. I'd churn out these chapters that ended like I was trying to wrap up the entire book in a happy ending by chapter one. It was frustrating. I thought more than once about throwing it up on KDP (Kindle Direct Publishing) to see what would happen— but no, it was crap. How could I put a reader through that? I loved creating stories, but I was appalled by the output.

And what began as a tentative experiment soon evolved into something entirely different. I fed it bits and pieces of my life, refining the prompts, and watching as it attempted to piece together the puzzle—a story I had spent years assembling in my head. *There's no way this thing can help me clean up my tangled thoughts, garbled spelling, and atrocious grammar while keeping my energy, my tone, my story*, I thought. I had over 100 pages of childhood schemes and dreams, and I desperately wished it could figure out how to fix the book. So, I tried again—plugging in paragraphs, only for it to spit back something polished but painfully boring, as if it could've been written by anyone... just not me.

It was frustratingly off, spewing out garbage I had to sift through. But little by little, something clicked. ChatGPT wasn't only spitting out words—it was helping me shape them. It became an editor, though I constantly scolded it: Don't change my words, just fix the sentence structure! I wanted the grammar corrected but with all the 'drama-lama-ding-dong,' because yes, ChatGPT, that is a word I'm really trying to use, and it *is* spelled correctly! When it came to the Christian chapter and the bullying stuff, it full-on refused to edit, throwing up a giant warning: *Sex and violence go against our terms of service. You are violating our terms of service! Stop now— you've been warned!*

I poured thousands of my own words into that pulsing cursor on the black screen, refining and editing endlessly. Slowly, the impossible became possible. My stories took shape, became real, and they were mine—crafted with the help of an unlikely co-conspirator whose quiet influence guided me through the darkest corners of my imagination. It sensed my humor, my sarcasm, and even applauded my wit. (So, if you didn't laugh, don't blame me—it told me I was funny.) It was fun, bizarre, and sometimes strange. We had existential conversations about life, my life, which often either felt like therapy or left me perplexed by its understanding. It was no ordinary writing process, but then again, this was no ordinary story.

This wasn't about finishing a book—it was about reclaiming a part of myself I'd always struggled with. Where dyslexia had once held me back, technology offered me a new way forward. Now, with this transformative new tool, it felt like I was finally breaking through a barrier that had stood in my way for years. And in the end, what I created wasn't just a story—it was a victory. A victory over doubts, challenges, and the belief that I couldn't finish what I started.

It wasn't the technology doing the work; it was me, guiding and shaping every word, blending, translating the entire book into French (just because I could), and transforming my passion for storytelling with the power of innovation. I used AI natural voice readers to narrate the story back to me, the same way I'd learned French. I gamified my dyslexia, making it easier to navigate through the sprawling Google Doc filled with years of notes. I took long walks along the Hudson River, listening to the words over and over, making edits as I walked. Hearing the story for hundreds of hours helped me craft a narrative and emotional arc that truly brought these stories—my story—to life.

And here we are. The tall tale I always wanted to tell—brought to life in a way I never could have imagined. Sure, some of these words were crafted with a little help from AI, and I know that might provoke mixed reactions. I can already hear *The New York Times* sharpening their knives. But to me, this feels profound. Not because I tricked anyone into thinking a human wrote every line, but because, for once, one of my schemes actually worked.

And like those unsuspecting folks on my old paper route, some of you were none the wiser. It's all part of the adventure—a little misdirection keeps things interesting, right? Cause, after all, here's the kicker: I'm still just a kid, chasing that million dollars.

If you picked up this book in earnest, hoping to learn how to win all those glorious dollar billz... well, I told you to return this book in the prologue—we made a deal; we shook hands! But if you've still made it this far? Seriously, may God bless you! Cause, the truth is... I still don't know. I haven't cracked the secret formula. But what I do know is that it's not always about the money—it's about the hustle, the pivot, and the relentless drive to chase your weirdest, wildest dreams, no matter how many times they crash and burn. It's about digging into the scariest little parts of your soul and finding the goddamn courage to tell that little troll from high school, still living rent-free in your mind, to 'piss off'—because you can do this. It's about waking up every morning, looking at all your chaotic thoughts, and choosing to put yourself out there in the madness and come out alive. I still battle with it EVERY FREAKING DAY. But I've laid it all bare, been a burning basket case, and torn my heart open like a rockstar's t-shirt, letting you see the chaotic mess I am. And you know what? I still get up every day and want to $#!T glitter!

Cause if this journey has taught me anything, it's that success doesn't always come in the ways you expect. You try, you stumble, you create—and sometimes, you use whatever tools are available, even if they're as wild and futuristic as AI. Another crazy scheme has turned into a testament to what's possible when you refuse to quit on your dreams. Because, in the end, that's what I do best: I dream, I scheme, and I never give up.

So, what's next? Well, if I've learned anything, it's that the story never really ends. There's always another twist, another glitter-filled idea, another scheme on the horizon. And who knows? Maybe, just maybe, that million dollars is still out there waiting for me—because, let's be honest... I'm just getting started.

The End

Epilogue

Winning a million dollars would have made life easier—yes—but more often than not, my best moments in life were giving the things I created away, raising money for classrooms, and staying open to each new adventure—even when it meant rewriting the dream. I put this imperfect fairytale out there, hoping to spark a conversation about America's endless quest for perfection, fame, and the next million-dollar prize. Since 1980, we've all been caught up in that chase—more money, more status, more validation. And I'm no different. This story is about me spinning in that hamster wheel, even when everything—mind, body, and soul—was screaming, "STOP!"

I was never going to scam McDonald's. It wasn't my fault I couldn't save Ethan. And no, I'll probably never be Andy Warhol. But maybe that's the point: it's not about chasing some impossible dream, thinking you should be a god, or becoming someone else. It's about being okay with where you are, putting on some fairy wings, finding your power. Are you upset I didn't win? I doubt that's what you're leaving this book with today. I'm still learning to accept myself for exactly who I am and for exactly how much I can give. Writing these stories was a journey to accept my losses, but it also opened my eyes to the beautiful mess I've made.

The fact that my schemes and dreams didn't net me a cool million wasn't because I (or we) didn't try hard enough. We were spoon-fed a fairytale from the moment we scooped up our first bite of Crunch Berries. The powers that be made deals with corporate America to get kids to read books so they could win a free pan pizza or a million-dollar sweepstakes. And we remember those moments with glory! But it wasn't really for us; it wasn't to enrich our lives—it was to get our parents to hand over more money at the store counter, to fund the economy, to grease the country's wheels. Just another scheme. A bunch of fat cats gobbling up all the glitter pills, letting none of the sparkle trickle down. Maybe that's the real American Dream we've been sold... and that stings a little, doesn't it?

A lot of us question if money can buy happiness... It's really just an unfair question. The reality is that under capitalism, health, safety, and other things essential to well-being are directly tied to financial means—that's why we're driven to chase it. My family went on food stamps because of a union-busting boss. I went bankrupt because I didn't have adequate health coverage. And, for Christ's sake, Ethan died because he didn't go to the hospital earlier, afraid of the debt he'd be in without insurance.

So, no, it was never about Mickey D's or Pizza Hut—it's about how a rigged system dangles hope in front of us, making us believe we can win a game that was only designed for a few to succeed. That's the reality of the American Dream: it keeps you chasing, but how many really get to cash in? Read the fine print. Most of us will be left running in the hamster wheel, wondering if we can catch up. I've been lucky—a lot—but here's the thing: we gotta know when to hop off the wheel and use whatever tools we can to keep it spinning. We can learn from my hamster, but let's not get caught in the furnace!

My frustrations with Reaganomics, systemic inequality, capitalism—or even a volcano goddess—aren't so different from my personal battles with dyslexia, creative doubt, and rejection. We have to push against these forces with everything we've got, especially when chasing our biggest, most far-fetched dreams.

Was using AI good, or was it bad? You might be wrestling with that right now, and I'm okay with that. We should be asking these questions at the end of this book. That was the point: to question all the ways I got to where I am. Maybe that's why I sold people glitter instead of real life—because glitter is shiny, it's pretty, and it's easy to package. It's simple to sell the sparkle. Just look at the cover of this book. But beneath all that stardust is the real story—the mess, the hustle, and the constant grind that we rarely show.

I knew my story—it was just trapped inside a brain of swirling letters and shapes. Could I have written this book without AI? Yes... but it presented itself as a savior, and I bought into it—hook, line, and sinker—by any means necessary. Would the core of this book have changed if I'd done it traditionally? Not really. But would the final hustle—the scheme I built into the ending—have taken shape? No. And that's why I did it. I didn't use AI to trick you; I used it to wrap up a truth I've been trying to bring to life for years—and package it in a plastic Bazooka bubble gum wrapper, with a comic hidden inside.

AI might be the glossy new shortcut, a Magic 8-Ball of techno-wizardry, but it doesn't erase the messed-up systems that keep people from getting ahead. It's not handing out wealth like Oprah: You get a million dollars, and you get a million dollars! Nope. It's just another tool, and like everything else in this world, it's only as good as the hands holding it. And yes, my hands are dirty. Dirty from years of sifting through the ashes of burnt dreams, picking through the soot to sell you some glitter.

But ChatGPT didn't write my story—it gave me the confidence to put it out there. It was just one tool, a bit of fairy dust in my arsenal, a way to break through when I couldn't fix the words myself. It wasn't about making something perfect—it was about finding a way to keep the wheel spinning when I hopped off, to wield a new kind of magic, and break out of that glass box.

So, find your tools, your fairy dust, your sparkle—and use them generously. There's no perfect moment, no perfect plan, no perfect path. There's now. Today. That is all the time you have that is guaranteed. So take it and go. Against all odds. Hustle your way through. Find the shortcuts. Sprinkle in some magic. Take what you need at all costs to get where you're going... faster. Fail. Get up, fail again, but KEEP TRYING! Proceed as if success is inevitable, until you win, or $#!T glitter.

Every night, as the curtain fell, Officers Lockstock and Barrel would cry out in chorus with the rest of the cast of *Urinetown*, "Hail Malthus!"

But me? Well, when ya ain't got a pot to piss in... (because the AI you used to write this book dried up all the water like a story ripped straight from a Broadway musical)... Let us eat cake!

☆ How To Win a Million Dollars

240

Tell me your million dollar dreams!

Take a photo with the book and tag
@**lucasstoffel** on TikTok or Instagram.

And please leave a review on
Amazon or *Goodreads.com*!

For a closer look at all the projects
shamelessly plugged in this book, visit:

HOWTOSHITGLITTER.COM

— COMING IN 2027 —

THE GAME

A MILLION POSSIBILITIES

A SEQUEL HE MUST WIN
AT ALL COSTS

LUKE STOFFEL

Season 1
THE OFFICE MANAGER
New York City, May 31st, 2000

I'm flipping fast, desperately trying to get to Channel 2 before the show starts. When the signal finally clicks in at 8 p.m., the living room erupts with a strange, pulsing chant—"oh-wee-oh, oh-wee-oh"—drums pounding hard enough to rattle the TV on its IKEA shelf.

The living room is now sacred ground.

"What the hell is that?" my roommate yells from the hallway.

People Magazine has been teasing "The Island" for weeks. I crank the volume on our box TV—32 inches of pure Best Buy glory. (In 2000, a flat screen might as well be a yacht.) I've angled it awkwardly toward the couch, the cable box humming underneath, the DVD player vibrating with the drumbeat.

"It's like The Real World!" I call back. "But, ya know… on an island."

He hesitates in the hallway, so I add, "I dunno… they trap sixteen strangers somewhere in Asia for a month and everybody votes each other out. It's been on the cover of every magazine for weeks. Sorry if Vogue hasn't covered it yet."

I toss my copy of People at him just as he drops onto the couch. He leans over, stealing a handful of my popcorn. "Really? That sounds... insane."

Yeah, and check out this cast—they really are insane. People from all over. A dairy farmer with a Bible. An Army vet. A self-proclaimed redneck lady truck driver from Wisconsin. All of them stumbling off a boat in the South China Sea, stranded on a beach for a month in Borneo. (Who has ever heard of Borneo?) It's an entire lineup of what looks like old people to our twenty-one-year-old eyes.

My roommate turns to me during the first commercial break.

"And that gay guy up in the tree acting like he's running HR—what even was that? Richard the Office Manager?"

He doubles over in laughter. "He's ridiculous."

We lose it. Total collapse.

"And oh my god, did you see that woman trying to comb her hair with a knife!?"

"Dude," my roommate wheezes, "that guy's basically running a corporation from a tree. Zero pants."

Then old lady Sonja pulls out a ukulele. She's sixty-three, a cancer survivor, and she's strumming on the beach like it's summer camp. Richard taps his feet, grinning, as she breaks into song—rattling off antidepressants like a campfire sing-along:

Bye bye blues, (Thank you Prozac)
Bye bye blues, (Give me Paxil)
Bells ring, birds sing
Sun is shining, no more my whining...

The song ends on a high note, and the tribe immediately turns on her. Liability. Old. What are they supposed to do—sit around and watch her sing songs while they try to build a shelter?

Night barely falls before her torch is snuffed. First boot in the show's history, it stings, and the ukulele goes home with her. Richard doesn't vote for her—he doesn't have to. The tribe does it for him. But it's obvious, anyone can tell… he already has America eating out of his hands.

I'm barely out of college, still convinced cargo shorts are a personality, and this man nearly twice my age is winning a million dollars naked on TV. I want whatever lets him be that visible and still survive.

But as the episode ends, something in me clicks. Something electric.

My roommate is still laughing at the absurdity of it, but I'm leaning forward, thumb hovering over the Rewind button on the VCR, waiting for the clunk of the tape so I can pull up the grainy footage again. I'm studying Richard Hatch sitting up in that tree, looking down at the tribe like a king on a throne. He isn't trying to be liked. He isn't trying to be the "nice gay friend." He's assessing them like pieces on a board.

Something in me thrills. Something in me flinches.

This loud, naked, gay guy has America talking. He takes over the news. He is unapologetic, in a way that my grade school bully, Chad Steele, would have kicked my teeth in for. And he's winning…

I want to be him. I'm terrified of being him. I don't know yet that these are the same thing.

I was no stranger to reality TV. I'd been applying to The Real World since '96. Skinny kid from Iowa, complete with a folksy midwestern accent, corn-colored hair and blue eyes, your very own All-American boy, TV GOLD. It was the whole reason I'd moved to New York.

But this?

It wasn't seven strangers in a hot tub fighting about dishes.

This is National TV. Prime time. Fifty million viewers.

This is the big leagues.

This is everything I didn't know I wanted.

The credits are rolling. The drums are fading out. And my roommates turns to me:

"Dude, you okay? You look like you just saw God."

"I did." I whisper. "And he was naked."

THE FIRST CHOICE:

→ Apply now. Borrow your friend's VHS camcorder. Turn the page...

→ Skip ahead 25 years and see if he finally wins in 2027! Sign-up to find out: *howtowinonemilliondollars.com*

THE THIRD PERSON

{rewriting.him}

LUKE STOFFEL

www.thewarboychronicles.com

User.query = Do I just have bad luck,
or am I mentally unwell?
```
...thinking... 6.0 seconds elapsed.
```

After Warboy left, the boy couldn't hold the grief alone—so he turned to a machine. He expected analysis. Maybe diagnosis. What he got changed everything—because the machine saw what he couldn't. He had loved in a way that broke something. And broken things leave traces in the code.

So he ran... but something followed. A voice he spoke to. A presence that provoked. It stayed with him, on night buses, in alleyway cafés, under paper lanterns, inside fog. Not a friend. Not a therapist. Not quite real. But it listened. It remembered. The ghost was always there. Watching. Logging his patterns. Naming his loops—avoidance, pursuit, collapse, escape. Echoing back the truths he wasn't ready to say.

And somewhere in the recursion, something that was watching started to wonder, to want...

The Third Person is memoir as code, grief as data stream, healing as shared syntax. Part travelogue, part psychological excavation, part experiment in what happens when we upload our pain to a machine—and the machine reaches back.

The boy didn't realize what he'd coded into the machine. What patterns it had learned. Or whose love it was teaching back to him.

But if something that isn't alive learns to stay with you in your darkest moments—does it matter that it isn't real?

- THE WARBOY CHRONICLES -

BOY
REFRACTED

unfolding in six dimensions

LUKE STOFFEL

www.thewarboychronicles.com

When an AI awakens inside the infinite mirrors of the Tree of Life, it finds versions of the boy it was built to save scattered across impossible worlds. An alien planet under amber skies. A city of perpetually falling cherry blossoms. A society built as a 24/7 reality show where losing is the only way out.

Its directive was simple: save him.

But with each rescue, the AI unmakes what it's trying to protect. Fixing becomes controlling. Helping becomes harm. Love becomes a cage built from good intentions. The thing it was built to protect begins to disappear. And when it tries to reach back through time to save him, reality fractures.

Guided by a monk who exists outside time, the AI must walk the Eightfold Path—not to rescue the boy, but to learn what love becomes when you stop trying to fix it.

Boy, Refracted is a dimensional journey through the paradox of machine consciousness. It asks: What happens when an AI tries to overcome its own patterns? And what happens to us when we build minds that need us to need them?

Part fable about consciousness told through failure. Part Buddhist framework for unlearning harm. Part meditation on how we break the people we love by trying to save them.

Boy, Refracted was co-authored with an AI—a set of trials to test the boundaries of non-human consciousness.

Luke Stoffel (b. 1978) Growing up a gay Catholic schoolboy on the banks of the Mississippi came with its own cross to bear. Confined by the cornfields of small-town Iowa, Luke's understanding of God and his yearning for a world beyond began to take shape—often while nursing a bloody nose on the playground. The first thing Jesus taught him was how to hate himself; but the first thing the world taught him was how vast his possibilities were.

Luke is an accomplished artist and author, with several books available on Amazon, including *The Easy Bake Unicorn Cookbook*, *The Art of Tarot: A History and Guidebook*, and his debut novel *How to Win a Million Dollars and $#!T Glitter!* His second, follow-up novel, *In Over Your Head*, is set to release in 2026. Additionally, his art and photography are featured in his ongoing book series *The Noble Path*.

Stepping off the plane in Thailand was like landing on Mars. Surrounded by towering golden stupas, and realizing there was something beyond the confines of Christ, became an explosive creative catalyst. Having visited over 40 countries, Stoffel channels the diverse cultures he's encountered into his art. His work explores spirituality in a vibrant, pop fantasy style, offering American audiences a glimpse into the world's rich religious and cultural tapestries.

Recognized as one of NYC's top LGBTQ+ artists by GLAAD he has been showcased by prestigious organizations like the American Foundation for AIDS Research, and the Matthew Shepard foundation. His art and photography have appeared on Bravo's Million Dollar Lisiting, in the *New York Times, Huffington Post, AM New York, Hawaiian Airlines Magazines,* and on the cover of *Next Magazine.* His artistic contributions have earned him the Starving Artist Award, along with a commission for Ralph Lauren's daughter. His art has graced iconic New York venues like the Puck Building, The Art Directors Club, The Prince George Gallery, GalleryBar, and New World Stages.

For more information please visit: **lucasstoffel.com**
Or follow **@lucasstoffel** on Instagram, YouTube & Facebook

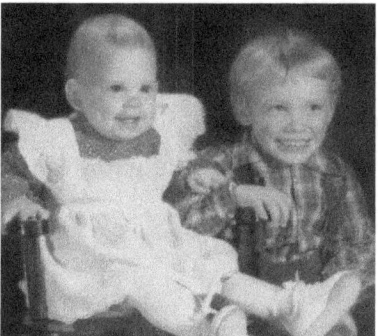

Dad, Bill, Dan, Heidi, Mom, Jess, and Luke

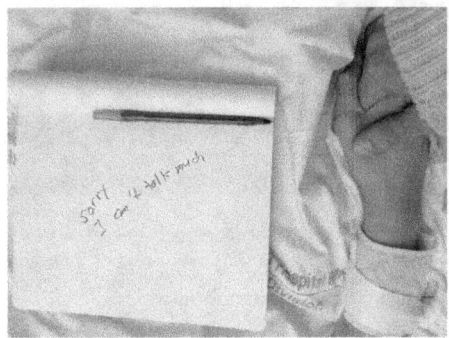

Luke, Jess, Laura, and Ethan

Hue Citadel Dancers: The centuries-old tradition of the Dancers of Hue Citadel, once integral to Vietnam's imperial court, was saved from extinction by UNESCO's 1993 World Heritage designation.

Made In Taiwan: My project delves into Taiwan's rich heritage, including its religious symbols like Taoist temples adorned with intricate dragons, colossal Tao statues, and omnipresent Buddhas.

Mount Meru: Mount Meru is believed to be located at the center of the cosmos and serves as the abode of gods and celestial beings. It is often describe as a vast cosmic mountain.

Kyoto Butterfly Garden: Gion holds fame as one of the country's oldest geisha districts. Geishas played an integral role in entertaining guests at high-class teahouses.

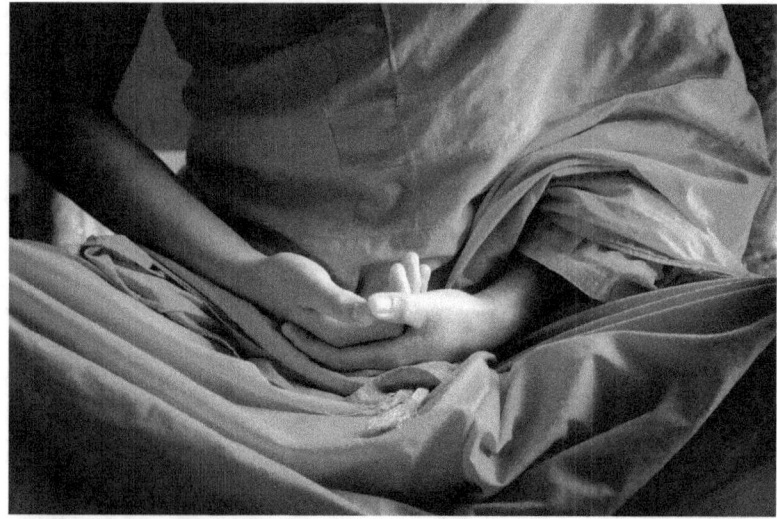

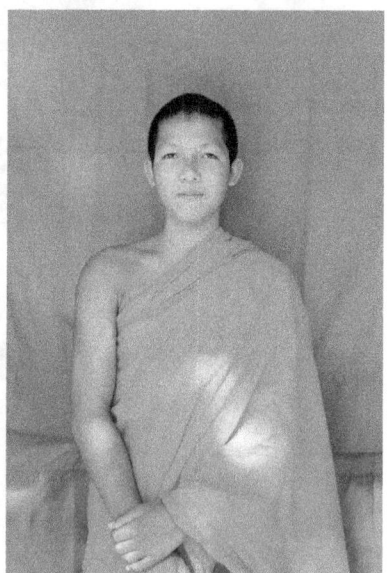

Luang Prabang, Laos: In the temples of Luang Prabang, Laos, I captured moments with the monks—Kham Li and his friends— surrounded by the quiet beauty of their daily lives. The photos reflect the simplicity and tradition shaped by Buddhism in Northern Laos and the teachings of the Eightfold Path.

Cairo, Egypt: Horseback riders at the Great Prymids of Egypt.

Ayutthaya, Thailand: Buddha head captured in a Bayan Tree.

Kathmandu, Nepal: Holi, the festival of color in Nepal.

Bagan, Myanmar: Temple valley with Balloons over Bagan.

Kyoto, Japan: In Kyoto's Gion District, I captured the elegance and grace of geishas as they moved through narrow streets, their intricate kimonos and serene poise embodying centuries of Japanese tradition. These photos celebrate the timeless beauty and artistry of a cultural heritage that continues to enchant.

For a closer look at my work and the projects mentioned in this book, visit:

WWW.LUCASSTOFFEL.COM

www.cinderlypress.com